ISBN: 9781314407112

Published by:
HardPress Publishing
8345 NW 66TH ST #2561
MIAMI FL 33166-2626

Email: info@hardpress.net
Web: http://www.hardpress.net

Purchased for the Library of
The University of Toronto
out of the proceeds of the fund
bequeathed by
B. Phillips Stewart, B.A., LL.B.
Ob. A.D. 1892.

THE ROMANTIC

NEW NOVELS

THE DUCHESS OF SIONA
ERNEST GOODWIN

THE VALLEY OF INDECISION
CHRISTOPHER STONE

MAINWARING
MAURICE HEWLETT

A TALE THAT IS TOLD
FREDERICK NIVEN

THE PEOPLE OF THE RUINS
EDWARD SHANKS

THE ROMANTIC
by
MAY SINCLAIR

Every kind and beautiful thing on earth has been made so by some cruelty.
Saying of the Romantic.

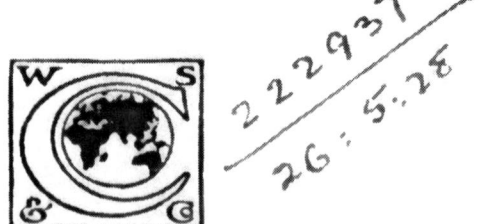

LONDON: 48 PALL MALL
W. COLLINS SONS & CO. LTD.
GLASGOW MELBOURNE AUCKLAND

PR
6037
I73 R6

Copyright 1920

CONTENTS

		PAGE
BOOK I.	CHARLOTTE REDHEAD	1
BOOK II.	JOHN RODEN CONWAY	57

BOOK I.—CHARLOTTE REDHEAD

BOOK I.—CHARLOTTE REDHEAD

I

They turned again at the end of the platform.

The tail of her long, averted stare was conscious of him, of his big, tweed-suited body and its behaviour, squaring and swelling and tightening in its dignity, of its heavy swing to her shoulder as they turned.

She could stave off the worst by not looking at him, by looking at other things, impersonal, innocent things: the bright, yellow, sharp-gabled station; the black girders of the bridge; the white signal post beside it holding out a stiff, black-banded arm; the two rails curving there, with the flat, white glitter and sweep of scythes; pointed blades coming together, buried in the bend of the cutting.

Small, three-cornered fields, clean-edged like the pieces of a puzzle, red brown and pure bright green, dovetailed under the high black bar of the bridge. She supposed you could paint that.

Turn.

Clear stillness after the rain. She caught herself smiling at the noise her boots made clanking on the tiles with the harsh, joyous candour that he hated. He walked noiselessly, with a jerk of bluff knickerbockered hips, raising himself on his toes like a cat.

She could see him moving about in her room, like that, in the half darkness, feeling for his things, with shamed, helpless gestures. She could see him tiptoeing down her staircase, furtive, afraid. Always afraid they would be found out.

That would have ruined him.

Oh, well—why should he have ruined himself for her? Why? But she had wanted, wanted to ruin herself for him, to stand, superb and reckless, facing the world with him. If that could have been the way of it——

Turn.

That road over the hill—under the yellow painted canopy sticking out from the goods station—it would be the Cirencester road, the

CHARLOTTE REDHEAD

Fosse Way. She would tramp along it when he was gone.

Turn.

He must have seen her looking at the clock. Three minutes more.

Suddenly, round the bend, under the bridge, the train.

He was carrying it off fairly well, with his tight red face and his stare over her head when she looked at him, his straight smile when she said, ' Good-bye and good-luck! '

And her silly hand clutching the window-ledge. She let go, quick, afraid he would turn sentimental at the end. But no; he was settling down heavily in his corner, blinking and puffing over his cigar.

That was her knapsack lying on the seat there. She picked it up and slung it over her shoulder.

Cirencester? Or back to Stow-on-the-Wold? If only he hadn't come there last night. If only he had let her alone.

She meditated. She would have to wire to Gwinnie Denning to meet her at Cirencester. She wondered whether Gwinnie's mother's lumbago would last over the week-end. It

THE ROMANTIC

was Friday. Perhaps Gwinnie had started. Perhaps there would be a wire from her at the hotel.

Going on to Cirencester when you wanted to be in Stow-on-the-Wold, what *was* it but a cowardly retreat? Driven out of Stow-on-the-Wold by Gibson? Not she!

Dusk at ten o'clock in the morning under the trees on the mile-long hill. You climbed up and up a steep green tunnel. The sun would be blazing at its mouth on the top. Nothing would matter. Certainly not this affair with Gibson Herbert. She could see clearly her immense, unique passion thus diminished.

Surprising what a lot of it you could forget. Clean forget. She supposed you forgot because you couldn't bear to remember.

But there were days that stood out; hours; little minutes that thrilled you even now and stung.

This time, two years ago, that hot August. The day in the office when everything went wrong all at once and the clicking of her typewriter maddened him, and he sent her out of his room.

The day when he kept her overtime. The others had gone and they were there by themselves, the big man in his big room and she in

CHARLOTTE REDHEAD

her den, the door open between. Suddenly she saw him standing in the doorway, looking at her. She knew then. She could feel the blood rushing in her brain; the stabbing click of the typewriter set up little whirling currents that swamped her thoughts.

Her wet fingers kept slipping from the keys. He came and took her in his arms. She lay back in his arms, crying. Crying because she was happy, because she knew.

She remembered now what he had said then. 'You must have known. You must have thought of me. You must have wanted me to take you in my arms.' And her answer. 'No. I didn't. I didn't think of it.'

And his smile. His unbelieving smile. He thought she was lying. He always thought people were lying. Women. He thought women always lied about what they wanted.

The first time. In her Bloomsbury room one evening, and the compact they made then, sitting on the edge of the sofa, like children, holding each other's hands and swearing never to go back on it, never to go back on themselves or on each other. If it ever had to end, a clean cut. No going back on that either.

THE ROMANTIC

The first night, in the big, gloomy bedroom of the hotel in Glasgow. The thick, gray daylight oozing in at the window out of the black street; and Gibson lying on his back, beside her, sleeping, the sheet dragged sideways across his great chest. His innocent eyelids.

And the morning after; the happiness. All day the queer, exalted feeling that she was herself, Charlotte Redhead, at last, undeceived and undeceiving.

The day his wife came into the office. Her unhappy eyes and small, sharp-pointed face, shrinking into her furs. Her name was Effie.

He had told her in the beginning that he had left off caring for his wife. They couldn't hurt her, she didn't care enough. She never had cared. There was another fellow. Effie would be all right.

Yet, after she had seen Effie it had never been the same thing. She couldn't remember, quite, how it had been.

She could remember the ecstasy, how it would come swinging through you, making you blind and deaf to impersonal, innocent things while it lasted. Even then there was always something beyond it, something you looked for and missed, something you thought would come that never came. There was something he did. She couldn't remember. That would be one of the things you wanted to forget. She saw his thick fingers at dessert, peeling the peaches.

Perhaps his way of calling her ' Poor Sharlie ? ' Things he let out ?—' I never thought I could have loved a girl with bobbed hair. A white and black girl.' There must have been other girls then. A regular procession. Before he married Effie.

She could see them. Pink and gold girls, fluffy and fat; girls with red hair; brown haired girls with wide, slippery mouths. Then Effie. Then herself, with her thick bobbed mane and white face. And the beautiful mouth he praised so.

Was it the disgust of knowing that you were only one of a procession ? Or was it that Effie's sad, sharp face slipped between ?

And the end of it. The breakdown, when Effie was ill.

His hysterical cries. ' My wife, Sharlie, my wife. We oughtn't to have done it. . . .

'. . . I can't forgive myself, Sharlie. I've been a brute, a beast, a stupid animal. . . .

THE ROMANTIC

'... When I think of what we've done to her—the little innocent thing—the awful unhappiness—I could kill myself.'

'Do you mean she knows?'

'She thinks. That's bad enough. If she knew, it would kill her.'

'You said she wouldn't care. You said there was another man.'

'There wasn't.'

'You lied, then?'

'Of course I lied. You wouldn't have come to me if I hadn't.'

'You told me you didn't care for her.'

He had met that with his 'Well—what did you want?'

She went over and over it, turning it round and round to see if there was any sort of light it would look a bit better in. She had been going to give him up so beautifully. The end of it was to have been wonderful, quiet, like a heavenly death, so that you would get a thrill out of that beauty when you remembered. All the beauty of it from the beginning, taken up and held together, safe at the end. You wouldn't remember anything else. And he had killed it, with his conscience, suddenly sick, whining, slobbering, vomiting remorse—turning on her.

'I can't think what you wanted with me. Why couldn't you have let me alone?'

Her own voice, steady and hard. 'If you feel dirty, go and wash yourself outside. Don't try and rub it off on me. I want to keep clean.'

'Isn't it a bit too late?'

'Not if you clear out at once. This minute.' He called her 'a cruel little devil.'

She could forgive him for that. She could forgive him ending it in any beastly way he liked, provided he did end it. But not last night. To come crawling back, three months after, wanting to begin again. Thinking it was possible.

There had been nothing worse than that. Except that one dreadful minute last year when he had wanted to raise her salary—afterwards—and she had said, 'What *for*?' And their faces had turned from each other, flaming with the fire of her refusal.

What had he really thought of her? Did he think she wanted to get anything out of their passion? What could you want to get out of it, or give, but joy? Pure joy. Beauty.

THE ROMANTIC

At the bend of the road the trees parted. A slender blue channel of sky flowed overhead between the green tops.

If not joy, then truth; reality. The clear reality of yourself, Charlotte Redhead. Of Gibson Herbert. Even now it would be all right so long as you knew what it was and didn't lie about it.

That evening in the office when he came to her—she could remember the feeling that shot up suddenly and ran over her and shook her brain, making her want him to take her in his arms. It was that. It had never been anything but that. She *had* wanted him to take her; and he knew it. Only, if he hadn't come to her and looked at her she wouldn't have thought about it; she would have gone on working for him without thinking. That was what he didn't know, what he wouldn't have believed if you had told him.

She had come to the top of the hill. At the cross-roads she saw the gray front of her inn, the bow window jutting, small black shining panes picked out with the clean white paint of the frame-work.

Upstairs their breakfast table stood in the

CHARLOTTE REDHEAD

window bow as they had left it. Bread he had broken on the greasy plate. His cup with the coffee he couldn't drink. Pathetic, if you hadn't remembered.

'You might as well. If it isn't you, it'll be another woman, Sharlie. If it isn't me, it'll be another man.'

That was what he had thought her.

It didn't matter.

II

She stood at the five roads, swinging her stick, undecided.

The long line of the beeches drew her, their heads bowed to the north as the south wind had driven them. The blue-white road drew her, rising, dipping and rising; between broad green borders under gray walls.

She walked. She could feel joy breaking loose in her again, beating up and up, provoked and appeased by the strong, quick movement of her body. The joy she had gone to her lover for, the pure joy he couldn't give her, coming back out of the time before she knew him.

Nothing mattered when your body was light and hard and you could feel the ripple and thrill of the muscles in your stride.

She wouldn't have to think of him again. She wouldn't have to think of any other man. She didn't want any more of that again, ever. She could go on and on like this, by herself, without even Gwinnie; not caring a damn.

CHARLOTTE REDHEAD

If she had been cruel—if she had wanted to hurt Effie. She hadn't meant to hurt her.

She thought of things. Places she had been happy in. She loved the high, open country.

Fancy sitting with Gibson in his stuffy office, day after day, for five years. Fancy going to Glasgow with him. Glasgow——

No. No.

She thought: 'I can pretend it didn't happen. Nothing's happened. I'm myself. The same me I was before.'

Suddenly she stood still. On the top of the ridge the whole sky opened, throbbing with light, immense as the sky above a plain. Hills —thousands of hills. Thousands of smooth curves joining and parting, overlapping, rolling together.

What did you want? What did you want? How could you want anything but this for ever?

Across the green field she saw the farm. Tall, long-skirted elms standing up in a row before the sallow ricks and long gray barns. Under the loaded droop of green a gray sharp-pointed gable, topped by a stone ball. Four Scotch firs beside it, slender and strange.

THE ROMANTIC

She stood leaning over the white gate, looking and thinking.

Funny things, colts grazing. Short bodies that stopped at their shoulders; long, long necks hanging down like tails, pushing their heads along the ground. She could hear their nostrils breathing and the scrinch, scrinch of their teeth tearing the grass.

You could be happy living on a farm, looking after the animals.

You could learn farming. People paid.

Suddenly she knew what she would do. She would do *that*. It wasn't reasonable to go on sitting in a stuffy office doing work you hated when you could pack up and go. She couldn't have stuck to it for five years if it hadn't been for Gibson—falling in love with him, the most unreasonable thing of all. She didn't care if you had to pay to learn farming. You had to pay for everything you learned. There were the two hundred pounds poor dear daddy left, doing nothing. She could pay.

She would go down to the farm now, this minute, and see if they would take her.

As she crossed the field she heard the farmyard gate open and shut.

CHARLOTTE REDHEAD

The man came up towards her in the narrow path. He was looking at her as he came, tilting his head back to get her clear into his eyes under the shade of his slouched hat.

She called to him. 'Is this your farm?' And he halted.

He smiled; the narrow smile of small, fine lips, with a queer, winged movement of the moustache, a flutter of dark down. She saw his eyes, hard and keen, dark blue, like the blade of a new knife.

'No. I wish it *was* my farm. Why?'

She could see now it wasn't. He was out tramping. The corner of a knapsack bulged over his right shoulder. Rough greenish coat and stockings—dust-coloured riding-breeches.

But there was something about him. Something tall and distant; slender and strange, like the fir-trees.

'Because whoever's farm it is I want to see him.'

'You won't see him. There isn't anybody there.'

'Oh.'

He lingered.

'Do you know who he is?' she said.

'No. I don't know anything. I don't even

THE ROMANTIC

know where I am. But I hope it's Bourton-on-the-Hill.'

'I'm afraid it isn't. It's Stow-on-the-Wold.'

He laughed and shifted his knapsack to his left shoulder, and held up his chin. His eyes slewed round, raking the horizon.

'It's all right,' she said. 'You can get to Bourton-on-the-Hill. I'll show you.' She pointed. 'You see where that clump of trees is—like a battleship, sailing over a green hill. That's about where it is.'

'Thanks. I've been trying to get there all afternoon.'

'Where have you come from?'

'Stanway. The other side of that ridge.'

'You should have kept along the top. You've come miles out of your way.'

'I like going out of my way. I did it for fun. For the adventure.'

You could see he was innocent and happy, like a child. She turned and went with him up the field.

She wouldn't go to Bourton-on-the-Hill. She would go back to the hotel and see whether there was a wire for her from Gwinnie. . . . He liked going out of his way.

CHARLOTTE REDHEAD

'I suppose,' he said, 'there's *something* the other side of that gate.'

'I hate to tell you. There's a road there. It's your way. The end of the adventure.'

He laughed again, showing small white teeth this time. The gate fell to with a thud and a click.

'What do I do now?'

'You go north. Straight ahead. Turn down the fifth or sixth lane on your right—you'll see the signpost. Then the first lane on your left. That'll bring you out at the top of the hill.'

'Thanks. Thanks most awfully.' He raised his hat, backing from her, holding her in his eyes till he turned.

He would be out of sight now at the pace he was going; his young slender, skimming stride.

She stood on the top of the rise and looked round. He was halting down there at the bend by the gray cone of the limekiln under the ash-tree. He had turned and had his face towards her. Above his head the battleship sailed on its green field.

He began to come back, slowly, as if he were looking for something dropped on his path; then suddenly he stopped, turned again, and was gone.

THE ROMANTIC

There was no wire from Gwinnie. She had waited a week now. She wondered how long it would be before Gwinnie's mother's lumbago gave in and let her go.

She knew it by heart now, the long, narrow coffee-room of the hotel. The draped chimney-piece and little oblong gilt-framed mirror at one end; at the other the bowed window looking west on to the ash-tree and the fields; the two straight windows between, looking south on to the street.

To-night the long table down the middle was set with a white cloth. The family from Birmingham had come. Father and mother, absurd pouter-pigeons swelling and strutting; two putty-faced, unmarried daughters, sulking; one married one, pink and proper, and the son-in-law, sharp-eyed and bald-headed. From their table in the centre they stared at her where she dined by herself at her table in the bow.

Two days. She didn't think she could bear it one day more.

She could see herself as she came down the room; her knitted silk sports' coat, bright petunia, flaming; thick black squares of her bobbed hair hanging over eyebrows and ears.

CHARLOTTE REDHEAD

And behind, the four women's heads turning on fat necks to look at her, reflected.

Gwinnie's letter was there, stuck up on the mantelpiece. Gwinnie could come at the week-end; she implored her to hang on for five days longer, not to leave Stow-on-the-Wold till they could see it together. A letter from Gibson, repeating himself.

The family from Birmingham were going through the door; fat faces straining furtively. If they knew—if they only knew. She stood, reading.

She heard the door shut. She could look in the glass now and amuse herself by the sight they had stared at. The white face raised on the strong neck and shoulders. Soft white nose, too thick at the nuzzling tip. Brown eyes straight and wide-open. Deep-grooved, clear-cut eyelids, heavy lashes. Mouth—clear-cut arches, moulded corners, brooding. Her eyes and her mouth. She could see they were strange. She could see they were beautiful.

And herself, her mysterious, her secret self, Charlotte Redhead. It had been secret and mysterious to itself once, before she knew.

She didn't want to be secret and mysterious. Of all things she hated secrecy and mystery.

THE ROMANTIC

She would tell Gwinnie about Gibson Herbert when she came. She would have to tell her.

Down at the end of the looking-glass picture, behind her, the bow window and the slender back of a man standing there.

She had got him clear by this time. If he went to-morrow, he would stay moving about for ever in your mind. The young body, alert and energetic; slender gestures of hands. The small, imperious head carried high. The spare, oval face with the straight-jutting, pointed chin. Honey-white face, thin dusk and bistre of eyelids and hollow temples and the roots of the hair. Its look of being winged, lifted up, ready to start off on an adventure. Hair brushed back in two sleek, dark wings. The straight, slender nose, with the close, upward wings of its nostrils—it wasn't Roman after all. Under it the winged flutter of his mouth when it smiled.

Black eyebrows almost meeting, the outer ends curling up queerly, like little moustaches. And always the hard, dark blue knife-blade eyes.

She knew his name the first day. He had told her. Conway. John Roden Conway.

The family from Birmingham had frightened

him. So he sat at her table in the bow. They talked. About places—places. Places they had seen and hadn't seen; places they wanted to see, and the ways you could get to places. He trusted to luck; he risked things; he was out, he said, for risk. She steered by the sun, by instinct, by the map in her head. She remembered. But you could buy maps. He bought one the next day.

They went for long walks together. She found out the field paths. And they talked. Long, innocent conversations. He told her about himself. He came from Coventry. His father was a motor-car manufacturer; that was why *he* liked tramping.

She told him she was going to learn farming. You could be happy all day long looking after animals. Swinging up on the big bare backs of the cart horses and riding them to water; milking cows and feeding calves. And lambs. When their mothers were dead. They would run to you then, and climb into your lap and sit there—sucking your fingers.

As they came in and went out together the family from Birmingham glared at them.

' Did you see how they glared ? '

' Do you mind ? ' he said.

THE ROMANTIC

'Not a bit.'

'No more do I. It doesn't matter what people like that do. Their souls are horrible. They leave a glairy trail everywhere they go. If they were dead—stretched out on their deathbeds—you'd see their souls, like long, fat, white slugs stretched out too, glued to their bodies. . . . You know what they think? They think we met each other here on purpose. They think we're engaged.'

'I don't care,' she said. 'It doesn't matter what they think.'

They laughed at the silliness of the family from Birmingham. He had been there five days.

'I—sa-ay——'

Gwinnie's voice drawled in slow, meditative surprise.

The brooding curiosity had gone out of her face. Gwinnie's face, soft and schoolgirlish between the fawn gold bands and plaited ear bosses of her hair, the pink, pushed out mouth, the little routing nose, the thick gray eyes, suddenly turned on you, staring.

Gwinnie had climbed up on to the bed to hear about it. She sat hunched up with her arms round her knees rocking herself on the end of her spine; and though she stared she still rocked. She was happy and excited because of her holiday.

'It can't make any difference, Gwin. I'm the same Charlotte. Don't tell me you didn't know I was like that.'

'Of course I knew it. I know a jolly lot more than you think, kid.'

'I'm not a kid—if you *are* two years older.'

'Why—you're not twenty-four yet. . . . It's the silliness of it beats me. Going off like that, with the first silly cuckoo that turns up.'

'He wasn't the first. He was the third—the third, I mean, that counted. There was poor Binky, the man I was engaged to. And Dicky Raikes; he wanted me to go to Mexico with him. Just for a lark, and I wouldn't. And George Corfield. *He* wanted me to marry him. And I wouldn't.'

'Why didn't you?'

'Because Dicky's always funny when you want to be serious, and George is always serious when you want to be funny. Besides, he's so good. His goodness would have been too much for me altogether. Fancy *beginning* with George.'

'This seems to have been a pretty rotten beginning anyway.'

THE ROMANTIC

'The beginning was all right. It's the end that's rotten. The really awful thing was Effie.'

'Look here——' Gwinnie left off rocking and swung herself to the edge of the bed. Her face looked suddenly mature and full of wisdom. 'I don't believe in that Effie business. You want to think you stopped it because of Effie; but you didn't. You've got to see it straight. . . . It was his lying and funking that finished you. He fixed on the two things you can't stand.'

The two things. The two things.

'I know what you want. You want to kill him in my mind, so that I shan't think of him any more. I'm not thinking. I only wanted you to know.'

'Does anybody else know?'

She shook her head.

'Well—don't you let them.'

Gwinnie slid to her feet and went to the looking-glass. She stood there a minute, pinning closer the crushed bosses of her hair. Then she turned.

'What are you going to do with that walking-tour johnnie?'

'John—Conway? You couldn't do anything

CHARLOTTE REDHEAD

with him if you tried. He's miles beyond all that.'

'All *what*?'

'The rotten things people do. The rotten things they think. You're safe with him, Gwinnie. Safe. Safe. You've only to look at him.'

'I *have* looked at him. Whatever you do, don't *tell* him, Sharlie!'

III

CHARLOTTE sat on the top of the slope in the field below Barrow Farm. John Conway lay at her feet. The tall beeches stood round them in an unclosed ring.

Through the opening she could see the farmhouse, three ball-topped gables, the middle one advancing, the front built out there in a huge doorplace that carried a cross-windowed room under its roof.

Low, heavy-browed mullions; the panes, black shining slits in the gray and gold of the stone. All their rooms. Hers and Gwinnie's under the near gable by the fir-trees, Mr and Mrs Burton's under the far gable by the elms, John's by itself in the middle, jutting out.

She could see the shallow garden dammed up to the house out of the green field by its wall, spilling trails of mauve campanula, brimming with pink phlox and white phlox, the blue spires of the lupins piercing up through the froth.

CHARLOTTE REDHEAD

Sunday evening, half an hour before milking-time. From September, nineteen-thirteen, to December—to March, nineteen-fourteen, to June—she had been at the farm nine months. June—May—April. This time three months ago John had come.

In the bottom of the field, at the corner by the yard-gate, under the elms, she could see Gwinnie astride over the tilted bucket, feeding the calves. It was Gwinnie's turn.

She heard the house door open and shut. The Burtons came down the flagged path between the lavender bushes, leaving them to their peace before milking time.

Looking down, she saw John's eyes blinking up at her through their lashes. His chest showed a red-brown V in the open neck of his sweater. He had been quiet a long time. His voice came up out of his quietness, sudden and queer.

'Keep your head like that one minute—looking down. I want your eyelids. . . . Now I know.'

'What?'

'What you're like. You're like Jeanne d'Arc. . . . There's a picture—the photo of a stone head, I think—in a helmet, looking down, with

THE ROMANTIC

big, dropped eyelids. If it isn't Jeanne it ought to be. Anyhow it's you. . . . That's what's been bothering me. I thought it was just because you had black hair bobbed like a fifteenth century page. But it isn't that. It's her forehead and her blunt nose, and her innocent, heroic chin. And the thick, beautiful mouth. . . . And the look—as if she could see behind her eyelids—dreadful things going to happen to her. All the butchery.'

'I don't see any dreadful things going to happen to me.'

'No. Her sight was second sight; and your sight is memory. You never forget things. . . . I shall call you Jeanne. You ought to wear armour and a helmet.' His voice ceased and began again. 'What are you thinking of?'

'I don't know. I don't think much, ever.'

She was wondering what *he* would think if he knew.

She wondered what the farm would be like without him. Would it be what it was last autumn and winter and in the spring before he came? But she had been happy all that time without him, even in the hard, frost-biting winter. When you had gone through that you knew the worst of Barrow Farm. It made your face coarse, though.

Joan of Arc was a peasant. No wonder she was beginning to look like her. If John went——

'John, shall you stay on here?'

'I don't know. I shall stick to farming if that's what you mean, though it isn't what I wanted.'

'*What* did you want?'

'To go into the Army.'

'Why didn't you, then?'

'They wouldn't have me. There's something wrong with my eyes. . . . So the land's got me instead.'

'Me too. We ought to have been doing this all our lives.'

'We'll jolly well have to. We shall never be any good indoors again.'

'Has old Burton said anything?'

'I'm getting on. I can drive as straight a furrow as any man in Gloucestershire. I've told my father that. He detests me; but he'd say you ought to work up from the plough-tail, if you *must* farm. He turned all of us through his workshops before he took us into the business. He liked to see us soaked in dirt and oil, crawling

THE ROMANTIC

on our stomachs under his engines. He'd simply love to see me here standing up to my knees in wet cow-dung.'

'He won't mind your leaving him?'

'Not if I make a good thing out of this. Anyhow he knows he can't keep me off it. If I can't fight, I'll farm. It's in my blood and nerves and memory. He sits there selling motor-cars, but his people were fighting men. They fought to get land; they fought to keep it. My mother's people were yeomen farmers. That's why my furrow's so straight.'

'And that's why you came here?'

'No. That isn't why.'

'Aren't you glad you came? Did you ever feel anything like the peace of it?'

'It's not the peace of it I want, Charlotte—Jeanne, I mean. It's the fight. Fighting with things that would kill you if you didn't. Wounding the earth to sow in it and make it feed you. Ploughing, Charlotte—Jeanne. Feeling the thrust and the drive through, and the thing listing over on the slope. Seeing the steel blade shine, and the long wounds coming in rows; hundreds of wounds, wet and shining.'

'What makes you think of wounds?'

'I don't know. I see it like that. Cutting through.'

'I don't see it like that one bit. The earth's so kind, so beautiful. And the hills—look at them, the clean, quiet backs smoothed with light. You could stroke them. And the fields, those lovely coloured fans opening and shutting.'

'They're lovely because of what's been done to them. If those hills had been left to themselves there'd have been nothing on them but trees. Think of the big fight with the trees, the hacking through, the cutting. The trunks staggering and falling. You'd begin with a little hole in the forest like that gap in the belt on the sky-line, and you'd go on hacking and cutting. You'd go on. . . . If you didn't those damned trees would come up and round you, and jam you between their trunks and crush you to red pulp. . . . Supposing this belt of beeches drew in and got tighter and tighter—No. There's nothing really kind and beautiful on this earth. Except your face. And even your face———'

'My face——?'

'*Could* be cruel. But it never will be. Something's happened to it. Some cruelty. Some damnable cruelty.'

THE ROMANTIC

'What makes you think so?'

'Every kind and beautiful thing on earth, Jeanne, has been made so by some cruelty.'

'That's all rot. Utter rot. You don't know what you're talking about. . . . It's milking time. There's Gwinnie semaphoring. Do you know old Burton's going to keep us on? He'll pay us wages from this quarter. He says we were worth our keep from the third day.'

'Do you want to stay on here?'

'Rather.'

'Very well then, so do I. That settles it.'

'Get up,' she said, 'and come along. Gwinnie's frantic.'

He sat up, bowed forwards, his hands hanging loose over his knees. She stood and looked down at him, at the arch of his long, slender back dropping to the narrow hips. She could feel the sudden crush of her breath in her chest and the sighing throb in her throat and her lips parting.

He grasped the hands she stretched out to him at arms' length. She set her teeth and pressed her feet to the ground, and leaned back, her weight against his weight, tugging.

He came to his feet, alert, laughing at the heavy strength of her pull. As they ran down the field he still held, loosely, like a thing forgotten, her right hand.

Through the long June night on her bed in the room under the gable—the hot room that smelt of plaster and of the apples stored in the loft behind it—she lay thinking.

Gwinnie had turned her back, burrowing into her pillow with a final shrug of her hips. She was asleep now in her corner.

'If I were you I wouldn't think about him, Sharlie'—she knew what Gwinnie meant. But thinking was one thing and caring was another. Thinking was the antidote to caring. If she had let her mind play freely over Gibson Herbert in the beginning—but Gibson stopped her thinking, and John Conway made her think. That was the difference.

There was nothing about John that was like Gibson. Not a look, not a gesture, not the least thought in his mind. His mind was like his body, clean and cold and beautiful. Set on fire only by dreams; loving you in a dream, a dream that burned him up and left him cold to you. Cold and clean.

There were things she laid up against him, the poor dear; a secret hoard of grievances now

THE ROMANTIC

clear to her in the darkness; she found herself turning them over and over, as if positively her mind owed his romantic apathy a grudge. Little things she remembered. Three things.

Yesterday in the hayfield, John pitching hay on to the cart, and she standing on the top of the load, flattening down the piles as he swung them up. Gwinnie came with a big fork, swanking, for fun, trying to pitch a whole haycock. In the dark of the room she could see Gwinnie's little body straining back from the waist, her legs stiffening, her face pink and swollen; and John's face looking at Gwinnie.

She shouted down at him, ' Why can't you *take* the damned thing? She'll break her back with it.' And he shouted up, ' That's her look-out.' (But he took it.) He didn't like Gwinnie.

That time. And the time Cowslip calved, the darling choosing the one night old Burton was away and Jim down with 'flu. She had to hold the lantern. Straw littered in the half-lighted shed. Cowslip swinging her bald-faced head round to you, her humble, sorrowful eyes imploring, between her groans and the convulsive heavings of her flanks. A noise between a groan and a bellow, a supreme convulsion. The dark wall, the white funnel of light from the lantern, and John's face in the flash. . . .

But he had been sorry for Cowslip. Going out with the lantern afterwards she had found him in the yard, by the wall, bent double, shivering and retching. And she had sung out to him, 'Buck up, John. She's licked it clean. It's the dearest little calf you ever saw.'

Pity. Pity could drag your face tight and hard, like Burton's, when his mare, Jenny, died of colic.

But before that—the night they went to Stow Fair together; crossing the street at the sharp turn by the church gate, something happened. They hadn't heard the motor-car coming; it was down on them, before they could see it, swerving round her side of the street. He had had his hand tight on her arm to steer her through the crowd. When the car came . . . when the car came . . . he let go and jumped clean to the curb. She could feel the splash-board graze her thigh, as she sprang clear of it, quick, like a dog.

She was sure he jumped first. She was sure he hadn't let go before the car came. She could

THE ROMANTIC

see the blaze of the lamps and feel his grip slacken on her arm.

She wasn't sure. He couldn't have jumped. He couldn't have let go. Of course he hadn't. She had imagined it. She imagined all sorts of things. If she could make them bad enough she would stop thinking about him; she would stop caring. She didn't want to care.

'Charlotte—when I die, that's where I'd like to be buried.'

Coming back from Bourton Market they had turned into the churchyard on the top of Stow hill. The long path went straight between the stiff yew cones through the green field set with graves.

'On the top, so high up you could almost breathe in your coffin here.'

'I don't want to breathe in my coffin. When I'm dead I'm dead, and when I'm alive I'm alive. Don't talk about dying.'

'Why not? Think of the gorgeous risk of it—the supreme toss up. After all, death's the most thrilling thing that happens.'

'Whose death?'

'My death.'

'Don't *talk* about it.'

'Your death, then.'
'Oh, mine——'
'Our death, Jeanne.'

He turned to her in the path. His mouth was hard now, but his eyes shone at her, smiling, suddenly warm, suddenly tender.

She knew herself then; she knew there was one cruelty, one brutality beyond bearing, John's death.

IV

John had gone away for a week.

If she could tire herself out, and not dream. In the slack days between hay-time and harvest she was never tired enough. She lay awake, teased by the rucking of the coarse, hot sheet under her back, and the sweat that kept on sliding between her skin and her nightgown. And she dreamed.

She was waiting in the beech ring on the top of the field. Inside the belt of the tree trunks a belt of stones grew up, like the wall of the garden. It went higher and higher and a hole opened in it, a long slit. She stuck her head through the hole to look out over the hills.

This was the watch-tower. She knew, as if she remembered it, that John had told her to go up and wait for him there; she was keeping watch for him on the tower.

Gray mist flowed over the field like water. He was down there in the field. If she went to him he would take her in his arms.

CHARLOTTE REDHEAD

She was walking now on the highway to Bourton-on-the-Hill. At the dip after the turn shallow water came out of the grass borders and ran across the road, cold to her naked feet. She knew that something was happening to John. He had gone away and she had got to find him and bring him back. She had got to find the clear hill where the battleship sailed over the field.

Instead of the ship she found the Barrow Farm beeches. They stood in a thick ring round a clearing of gray grass and gray light. John was standing there with a woman. She turned and showed her sharp face, the colour of white clay, her long, evil nose, her eyes' tilted corner and the thin tail of her mouth, writhing. That was Miss Lister, who had been in Gibson's office. She had John now.

Forms without faces, shrouded white women larvæ slipped from the black grooves of the beech trunks; they made a ring round him with their bodies, drew it in tighter and tighter. The gray light beat like a pulse with the mounting horror.

She cried out his name, and her voice sounded tragic and immense; sharp like a blade of lightning screaming up to the top of the sky.

THE ROMANTIC

A black iron curtain crashed down before her and cut off the dream.

Gwinnie looked up over the crook of her knee from the boot she was lacing.

'You made no end of a row in your sleep, Sharlie.'

She had dreamed about him again, the next night. He was walking with her on the road from the town to the farm. By the limekiln at the turn he disappeared. He had never been there, really.

She had gone out to look for him. The road kept on curling round like a snake, bringing her back and back to the white gate of the farm.

When she got through the gate she stepped off the field on to the low bridge over a black canal. The long, sharp-pointed road cut straight as a dyke through the flat fields, between two lines of slender trees, tall poles with tufted tops.

She knew she was awake now because the light whitened and the wind moved in the tree tufts and the road felt hard under her feet. When she came to the village, to the long gray walls with narrow shutters, she knew John was there. He came down the street towards the canal bridge. A group of women and children walked with him, dressed in black. Dutch women. Dutch babies. She could see their overalls and high caps and large, upturned shoes very black and distinct in the white light. This was real.

They pointed their fingers and stared at her with secretive, inimical faces. Terror crept in over the street, subtle, drifting and penetrating like an odour.

John's face was happy and excited; that was how she knew him. His face was real, its happiness and excitement were real. But as he passed her it changed; it turned on her with a look she didn't know. Eyes of hatred, eyes that repudiated and betrayed her.

The third night; the third dream.

She had lost John and was looking for him; walking a long time through a country she could no longer see or remember. She came out of blank space to the river bridge and the red town. She could see the road switchbacking over the bridge and turning sharp and slanting up the river bank to the ramparts.

Red fortresses above the ramparts, a high, red town above the fortresses, a thin, red tower above the town. The whole thing looked dangerous and unsteady, as if any minute it

THE ROMANTIC

would topple over. She knew John was there. Something awful was happening to him, and he wanted her.

When she stepped on the bridge the river swelled and humped itself up to the arch. It flooded. The bridge walls made a channel for the gush. It curled over the bank and came curving down the slant road from the ramparts, heavy and clear, like melted glass.

She climbed up and up through the water, and round behind the fortress to the street at the top. She could see the thin tower break and lean forward like a red crane above the houses. She had to get to the top before the street fell down. John was shut up in the last house. She ran under the tower as it fell.

The house stood still, straight and tall. John was lying in the dark room behind the closed shutters. He wanted her. She could hear him calling to her, 'Jeanne! Jeanne!' She couldn't see in. She couldn't open the door.

'Jeanne!'

The wall split off and leaned forward.

She woke suddenly to the tapping and splashing of the rain.

V

Feeding time and milking time were done; in his jutting room over the doorplace John was washing and dressing for Sunday evening. He called out to her through his window, 'Go up to our seat and wait for me there.'

He had come back again, suddenly, that morning, a day before they had expected him.

Charlotte came out of the hot field into the cool room of the beech ring. She sniffed up the clean, sharp smell of sap from the rough seat that she and John had put up there, sawing and hacking and hammering all Sunday afternoon. Every evening when the farm work was done they would sit there together, inside the round screen of the beeches.

The farm people wouldn't disturb them; not even Mr Burton, now, looking in, smiling the fat, benevolent smile that blessed them, and going away; the very calves were so well used to them that they had left off pushing their noses through the tree trunks and staring.

THE ROMANTIC

John's window faced her where she sat; she could see his head passing and passing across the black window space. To her sharp, waiting soul Barrow Farm took on a sudden poignant and foreign beauty. The house was yellow where the rain had soaked into it, gold yellow like a sun-struck southern house, under the black plume of the firs, a yellow that made the sky's blue solid and thick. The grass, bright green after the rain, stretched with the tight smoothness of velvet over the slopes and ridges of the field. A stripe of darker green, where their feet had trodden down the blades, led straight as a sheep's track from the garden gate to the opening of the ring.

To think that she had dreamed bad dreams in a place like this. She thought: 'There must be something wrong about me, anyhow, to dream bad dreams about John.'

John was coming up the field, walking slowly, his hands thrust in his pockets, his eyes fixed steadily on a point in front of him that his mind didn't see, drawn back in some intense contemplation. He strolled into the ring so slowly that she had time to note the meditative gestures of his shoulders and chin. He stood beside her, very straight and tall, not speaking, still hiding his hands in his pockets, keeping up to the last minute his pose of indestructible tranquillity. He was so close that she could hear his breathing and feel his coat brushing her shoulder.

He seated himself, slowly, without a break in the silence of his meditation.

She knew that something wonderful and beautiful was going to happen. It had happened; it was happening now, growing more certain and more real with every minute that she waited for John to say something. If nothing changed, if this minute that she was living now prolonged itself, if it went on for ever and ever, that would be happiness enough.

If she could keep still like this for ever. Any movement would be dangerous. She was afraid almost to breathe.

Then she remembered. Of course, she would have to *tell* him.

She could feel the jerk and throb in John's breathing, measuring off the moments of his silence. Her thoughts came and went. ' When he says he cares for me I shall have to tell him.' —' This is going on for ever. If he cared for me he would have said it before now.' —' It doesn't matter. He can care or not as he likes. Nothing can stop my caring.'

THE ROMANTIC

Then she was aware of her will, breaking through her peace, going out towards him, fastening on his mind to make him care; to make him say he cared, now, this minute. She was aware of her hands, clenched and unclenched, pressing the sharp edge of the seat into their palms as she dragged back her will.

She was quiet now.

John was looking at his own loose, clasped hands and smiling. 'Yes,' he said, 'yes, yes.' It was as if he had said, 'This will go on. Nothing more than this can ever happen. But as long as we live it will go on.'

She had a sense almost of relief.

'Charlotte——'

'John——'

'You asked me why I came here. You must have known why.'

'I didn't. I don't.'

'Can't you think?'

'No, John. I've left off thinking. *My* thinking's never any use.'

'If you *did* think you'd know it was you.'

'*Me?*'

'If it wasn't you just at first it was your face. There are faces that do things to you, that hurt you when they're not there. Faces of people you don't know in the least. You see them once and they never let you alone till you've seen them again. They draw you after them, back and back. You'd commit any sin just to see them again once. . . .

'. . . You've got that sort of face. When I saw you the first time—do you remember? You came towards me over that field. You stopped and spoke to me.'

'Supposing I hadn't?'

'It wouldn't have mattered. I'd have followed you just the same. Wherever you'd gone I'd have gone too. I very nearly turned back then.'

She remembered. She saw him standing in the road at the turn.

'I knew I had to see you again. But I waited two days to make sure. Then I came. . . .

'. . . And when I'd gone I kept on seeing your face. It made me come back again. And the other day—I tried to get away from you. I didn't mean to come back; but I had to. I can't stand being away from you. And yet . . .

'. . . Oh, well—there it is. I had to tell you. . . . I couldn't if I didn't trust you.'

'You tried to get away from me. You didn't mean to come back.'

'I tell you I *had* to. It's no use trying.'

THE ROMANTIC

'But you didn't *want* to come back. . . . *That's* why I dreamed about you.'

'Did you dream about me?'

'Yes. Furiously. Three nights running. I dreamed you'd got away and when I'd found you a black thing came down and cut you off. I dreamed you'd got away, again, and I met you in a foreign village with a lot of foreign women, and you looked at me and I knew you hated me. You wouldn't know me. You went by without speaking and left me there.'

'My God—you thought I could do that?'

'I dreamed it. You don't think in dreams. You feel. You see things.'

'You see things that don't exist, that never can exist, things you've thought about people. If I thought that about myself, Jeanne, I'd blow my brains out now, so that it shouldn't happen.'

'That wasn't the worst dream. The third was the worst. You were in a dreadful, dangerous place. Something awful was happening, and you wanted me, and I couldn't get to you.'

'No, that wasn't the worst dream. I *did* want you, and you knew it.'

She thought: 'He cares. He doesn't want to care, but he does. And he trusts me. I shall have to tell him. . . .

CHARLOTTE REDHEAD

'There's something,' she said, 'I've got to tell you.'

He must have known. He must have guessed.
He had listened with a gentle, mute attention, as you listen to a story about something that you remember, that interests you still, his eyes fixed again on his own hands, his clear, beautiful face dreamy and inert.

'You see,' he said, 'you did trust me. You wouldn't tell me all that if you didn't.'

'Of course I trust you. I told you because you trusted *me*. I thought—I thought you ought to know. I dare say you did know—all the time.'

'No. No, I didn't. I shouldn't have believed it was in you.'

'It isn't in me now. It's gone clean out of me. I shall never want that sort of thing again.'

'I know *that*.' He said it almost irritably. 'I mean I shouldn't have thought you could have cared for a brute like that. . . . But the brutes women *do* care for . . .'

'I suppose I did care. But I don't feel as if I'd cared. I don't feel as if it had ever really happened. I can't believe it did. You see, I've forgotten such a lot of it. I couldn't have believed

THE ROMANTIC

that once, that you could go and do a thing like that and forget about it. You'd have thought you'd remember it as long as you lived.'

'You couldn't live if you remembered. . . .'

'Oh, John, do you think it was as horrible as all that?'

His face moved, flashed into sudden passion.

'I think *he* was as horrible as that. He makes it horrible—inconceivably horrible.'

'But—he wasn't.'

'You've told me. He was cruel to you. And he lied and funked.'

'It wasn't like him—it wasn't *like* him to lie and funk. It was my fault. I made the poor thing jumpy. I let him run such whopping risks. *The* horrible thing is thinking what I made him.'

'He was a liar and a coward, Charlotte; a swine.'

'I tell you he *wasn't*. Oh, why are we so beastly hard on each other? Everybody's got their breaking-point. I don't lie about the things he lied about; I don't funk the things he funked. But when my time comes, I dare say I shall funk and lie.'

'Charlotte—are you sure you don't care for him?'

CHARLOTTE REDHEAD

'Of course I'm sure. I told you I'd forgotten all about it. *This* is what I shall remember all my life. Your being here, my being with you. It's the *real* thing.'

'You wouldn't want to go back?'

'To him?'

'No. To that sort of thing.'

'You mean with—just anybody?'

'I mean with—somebody you cared about. Could you do without it and go on caring?'

'Yes. If *he* could. If he could go on. But he wouldn't.'

'" He " wouldn't, Charlotte. But *I* would. . . . You know I *do* care for you?'

'I thought you *did*—I mean I thought you were beginning to. That's why I told you what happened, though I knew you'd loathe me.'

'I don't. I'm glad you told me. I'm glad it happened. I mean I'm glad you worked it off on him. . . . You got it over; you've had your experience; you know all about it; you know how long that sort of thing lasts and how it ends. The baseness, the cruelty of it. . . . I'm like you, Charlotte, I don't want any more of it. . . . When I say I care for you I mean I want to be with you, to be with you *always*. I'm not happy when you're not there. . . .

THE ROMANTIC

'... I say, I wish you'd leave this place and come away and live with me somewhere.'

'Where?'

'There's my farm. My father's going to give me one if I stick to this job. We could run it together. There are all sorts of jolly things we could do together.... Would you like to live with me, Charlotte, on my farm?'

'Yes.'

'I mean—live with me without *that*.'

'Yes; without that.'

'It isn't that I don't care for you. It's because I care so awfully, so much more than anybody else could. I want to go on caring, and it's the only way. People don't know that. They don't know what they're destroying with their blind rushing together. All the delicate, exquisite sensations. Charlotte, I can get all the ecstasy I want by just sitting here and looking at you, hearing your voice, touching you—like this.' His finger-tips brushed the bare skin of her arm. ' Even thinking of you....

'... And all that would go. Everything would go.... But our way—nothing could end it.'

'I can see one thing that would end it. If you found somebody you really cared about.'

'Oh *that*—you mean if I—it wouldn't happen, and if it did, what difference would it make?'

'You mean you'd come back?'

'I mean I shouldn't have left you.'

'Still, you'd have gone to her. John, I don't think I could bear it.'

'You wouldn't have to bear it long. It wouldn't last.'

'Why shouldn't it?'

'Because—you don't understand, Charlotte—if I know a woman wants me, it makes me loathe her.'

'It wouldn't, if you wanted *her*.'

'That would be worse. I should *hate* her then if she made me go to her.'

'You don't know.'

'Oh, don't I!'

'You can't, if you feel like that about it.'

'You say you feel like that about it yourself.'

'That's because I've been through it.'

'Do you suppose,' he said, 'I haven't?'

BOOK II.—JOHN RODEN CONWAY

BOOK II.—JOHN RODEN CONWAY

VI

It was an hour since they had left Newhaven.

The boat went steadily, inflexibly, without agitation, cutting the small, crisp waves with a sound like the flowing of stiff silk. For a moment after the excited rushing and hooting of the ambulance car, there had been something not quite real about this motion, till suddenly you caught the rhythm, the immense throb and tremor of the engines.

Then she knew.

She was going out, with John and Gwinnie Denning and a man called Sutton, Dr Sutton, to Belgium, to the war. She wondered whether any of them really knew what it would be like when they got there. She was vague, herself. She thought of the war mostly in two pictures: one very distant, hanging in the air to her right, colourless as an illustration in the papers, gray figures tumbled in a gray field, white puff-bursts

THE ROMANTIC

of shrapnel in a gray sky: and one very near; long lines of stretchers, wounded men and dead men on stretchers, passing and passing before her. She saw herself and John carrying a stretcher, John at the head and her at the foot, and Gwinnie and Dr Sutton with another stretcher.

Nothing for her and John and Gwinnie but field work; the farm had spoiled them incurably for life indoors. But it had hardened their muscles and their nerves, it had fitted them for the things they would have to do. The things they would have to see. There would be blood; she knew there would be blood; but she didn't see it; she saw white, very white bandages, and grayish white, sallow-white faces that had no features that she knew. She hadn't really thought so very much about the war; there had been too many other things to think about. Their seven weeks' training at Coventry, the long days in Roden and Conway's motor works, the long evenings in the ambulance classes; field practice in the meadow that John's father had lent to the Red Cross; runs along the Warwickshire roads with John sitting beside her, teaching her to steer and handle the heavy ambulance-car. An endless preparation.

JOHN RODEN CONWAY

And under it all, like a passion, like a hidden illness, their impatience, their intolerable longing to be out there.

If there had been nothing else to think about there was John. Always John. Not that you could think about him without thinking about the war; he was so thoroughly mixed up with it; you couldn't conceive him as left out of it or as leaving himself out. It had been an obsession with him, to get into it, to get into it at once, without waiting. That was why there were only four of them. He wouldn't wait for more volunteers. They could get all the volunteers they wanted afterwards; and all the cars, his father would send out any number. She suspected John of not really wanting the volunteers, of not even wanting Gwinnie and Dr Sutton. She could see he would have liked to have gone with her alone. Queer, that so long as she had thought he would be going without her, she had been afraid; she had felt certain he would be killed or die of wounds. The one unbearable thing was that John should die. But after it had been settled that she was to go out with him as his chauffeur she hadn't been afraid any more. It was as if she knew that she would keep him safe. Or perhaps all the

THE ROMANTIC

time she had been afraid of something else. Of separation. She had had visions of John without her in another country; they were coloured, vaguely, with the horror of her dreams. It had been just that. Anyhow, she hadn't thought any more about John's dying.

It was the old man, his father, who had made her think of it now.

She could see him, the gray, kind, silent man, at the last minute, standing on the quay and looking at John with a queer, tight look as though he were sorry about something—oh, but unbearably sorry about something he'd thought or said or done. He was keeping it all in, it was a thing he couldn't speak about, but you could see it made him think John wasn't coming back again.

He had got it into his head that she was going out because of John. She remembered, before that, his kind, funny look at her when he said to John, ' Mind you take care of her,' and John's ' No fear,' and her own, ' *That's* not what he's going out for.' She had a slight pang when she thought of John's father. He had been good to Gwinnie and to her at Coventry.

But as for going out because of John, whether he went or not she would have had to go, keen, so keen that she hated those seven weeks at Coventry, although John had been there.

With every thud of the engines her impatience was appeased.

And all the time she could hear Gwinnie's light, cool voice explaining to Dr Sutton that the British Red Cross wouldn't look at them and their field ambulance, but the Belgians, poor things, you know, weren't in a position to refuse. They would have taken almost anything.

Her mind turned to them: to Gwinnie, dressed in their uniform, khaki tunic and breeches and puttees, her fawn-coloured overcoat belted close round her to hide her knees. Gwinnie looked stolid and good, with her face, the face of an innocent, intelligent routing animal, stuck out between the close wings of her motor-cap and the turned-up collar of her coat. She would go through it all right. Gwinnie was a little plodder. She would plod through the war as she had plodded through her training, without any fear of tests.

And Dr Sutton. From time to time she caught him looking at her across the deck. When Gwinnie's talk dropped he made no effort to revive it, but stood brooding: a square, thick-

THE ROMANTIC

set man. His head leaned forward a little from his heavy shoulders in a perpetual short-sighted endeavour to look closer; you could see his eyes, large and clear under the watery wash of his glasses. His features, slightly flattened, were laid quietly back on his composed, candid face; the dab of docked moustache rising up in it like a strange note of wonder, of surprise.

There, he was looking at her again. But whether he looked or listened, or stood brooding, his face kept still all the time, still and sad. His mouth hardly moved as he spoke to Gwinnie.

She turned from him to the contemplation of their fellow passengers. The two Belgian boy scouts in capes and tilted caps with tassels bobbing over their foreheads; they tramped the decks, seizing attention by their gay, excited gestures. You could see that they were happy.

The group, close by her in the stern, establishing itself there apart, with an air of righteous possession: five, six, seven men, three young, four middle-aged, rather shy and awkward, on its fringe. In its centre two women in slender tailor-made suits and motor veils, looking like bored, uninterested travellers used to the adventure.

JOHN RODEN CONWAY

They were talking to a little man in shabby tweeds and an olive green velvet hat too small for his head. His smooth, innocent pink face carried its moustache like an accident, a mistake. Once, when he turned, she met the arched stare of small china-blue eyes; it passed over her without seeing, cold, dreamy, indifferent.

She glanced again at his women. The tall one drew you every time by her raking eyes, her handsome, arrogant face, the gesture of her small head, alert and at the same time set, the predatory poise of an enormous bird. But the other one was—rather charming. Her features had a curious, sweet bluntness; her eyes were decorations, deep-set blue in the flushed gold of her sunburn. The little man straddled as he talked to them, bobbing forward now and then with a queer, jerking movement from his hips.

She wondered what they were, and decided that they were part of the Commission for Relief in Belgium, bound for Ostend.

All those people had the look that John had, of having found what they had wanted, of being satisfied, appeased. Even Sutton had it, lying on the top of his sadness, like a light. They felt precisely as she was feeling—all those people.

THE ROMANTIC

And through her wonder she remained aware of John Conway as he walked the deck, passing and passing in front of her.

She got up and walked with him.
The two women stared at them as they passed. One, the tall one, whispered something to the other.

'John—do my knees show awfully as I walk?'
'No. Of course they don't. Gwinnie's do. She doesn't know what to do with them.'

He looked down at her and smiled.
'I like you. I like you in that cap. You look as if you were sailing fast against a head wind, as if you could cut through anything.'

Their turn brought them again under the women's eyes. He took her arm and drew her aside to the rail of the boat's stern. They stood there, watching the wake boiling and breaking and thinning, a white lace of froth on the glassy green. Sutton passed them.

'What's the matter with him?' she said.
'The War. He's got it on his mind. It's no use taking it like that, Jeanne, as one consummate tragedy. . . . How are *you* feeling about it?'

'I don't think I'm feeling anything—except

wanting to get there. And wanting—wanting frightfully—to help.'

'Unless you can go into it as if it was some tremendous, happy adventure—that's the only way to take it. I shouldn't be any good if I didn't feel it was the most *romantic* thing that ever happened to me. . . . To have let everything go, to know that nothing matters, that it doesn't matter if you're killed, or mutilated. . . . Of course I want to help, but that would be nothing without the gamble. The danger.'

He stopped suddenly in his turning and held her with his shining, excited eyes.

'War's the most romantic thing that ever happened. . . . False romance, my father calls it. Jolly little romance about *him*. He'll simply make pots of money out of the war, selling motors to the Government.'

'It's rather—romantic of him to give us those two ambulances, and pay for us.'

'*Is* it ? Think of the kudos he gets out of it, and the advertisement for Roden and Conway, the stinking paragraphs he'll put in the papers about himself: "His second son, Mr John Roden Conway, is taking out two Roden field-ambulance cars which he will drive himself."

THE ROMANTIC

—" Mr John Roden Conway and his field-ambulance car. A Roden, 30 horse-power." He makes me sick.'

She saw again, with a renewal of her pang, the old man, the poor, kind man. Perhaps he wouldn't put the paragraphs in the papers.

'False romance? He lies. There's no such thing as false romance. Romance is a state of mind. A state of mind can't be false, or true. It simply exists. It hasn't any relation to reality. It *is* reality, the most real part of us. When it's dead we're dead.'

'Yes.'

But it was funny to *talk* about it. About romance and danger. It made her hot and shy. She supposed that was because she couldn't take things in. Her fatheadedness. It was easy not to say things if you didn't feel them. The more John felt them the more he had to say them. Besides, he never said them to anybody but her. It was really saying them to himself, a quiet, secret thinking.

He stood close, close in front of her, tall and strong and handsome in his tunic, knee breeches, and puttees. She could feel the vibration of his intense, ardent life, of his excitement. And suddenly, before his young manhood, she had it again, the old feeling, shooting up and running over her, swamping her brain. She wondered with a sort of terror whether he would see it in her face, whether if she spoke he would hear it thickening her throat. He would loathe her if he knew. She would loathe herself if she thought she was going into the war because of that, because of him. Women did. She remembered Gibson Herbert. Glasgow. . . . But this was different. The sea was in it, magic was in it, and romance. And if she had to choose between John and her wounded, it should not be John. She had sworn that before they started. Standing there close beside him she swore again, secretly to herself, that it should not be John.

John glanced at Sutton as he passed them.

'I'd give my soul to be a surgeon,' he said. 'That's what I wanted.'

'You wanted to be a soldier.'

'It would have been the next best thing. . . . Did you notice in the lists the number of Army medical men killed and missing? Out of all proportion. That means that they're as much exposed as the combatants. More, really. . . .

'. . . Jeanne—do you realise that if we've any luck, any luck at all, we shall take the same risks?'

THE ROMANTIC

'It all very well for us. If it was only being killed—but there's killing.'

'Of course there's killing. If a man's willing to be killed he's jolly well earned his right to kill. It's the same for the other johnnie. If your life doesn't matter a hang, his doesn't either. He's got his feeling. He's got his romance. If he hasn't——'

'Yes—if he hasn't?'

'He's better dead.'

'Oh, no; he might simply go slogging on without feeling anything, from a sense of duty. That would be beautiful; it would be *the* most beautiful thing.'

'There you are, then. His duty's his romance. You can't get away from it.'

'No.'

But she thought: Supposing he went, loathing it, shivering, sick? Frightened. Well, of course, it would be there too, simply because he *went*; only you would feel it, not he.

Supposing he didn't go, supposing he stuck, and had to be pushed on, by bayonets, from behind? It didn't bear thinking of.

John hadn't thought of it. He wouldn't. He couldn't see that some people were like that.

JOHN RODEN CONWAY

'I don't envy,' he said, 'the chaps who come out to soft jobs in this war.'

They had found the little man in tweeds asleep behind the engine house, his chin sunk to his chest, his hands folded on his stomach. He had taken off his green velvet hat, and a crest of grayish hair rose up from his bald forehead, light and fine.

The sun was setting now. The foam of the wake had the pink tinge of red wine spilt on a white cloth; a highway of gold and rose, edged with purple, went straight from it to the sun.

After the sunset, land, the sunk lines of the Flemish coast.

There was a stir among the passengers; they plunged into the cabins and presently returned, carrying things. The groups sorted themselves, the Commission people standing apart with their air of arrogance and distinction. The little man in tweeds had waked up from his sleep behind the engine house, and strolled with a sort of dreamy swagger to his place at their head. Everybody moved over to the starboard side.

They stood there in silence watching the white walls and domes and towers of Ostend. Charlotte and Conway had moved close to each

THE ROMANTIC

other. She looked up into his face, searching his thoughts there. Suddenly from somewhere in the bows a song spurted and dropped and spurted again, and shot up in the sillness, slender and clear, like a rod of white water. The Belgian boys were singing the Marseillaise. On the deck their feet beat out the thud of the march.

Charlotte looked away.

VII·

'Nothing,' Charlotte said, 'is going to be worse than this.'

It seemed to her that they had waited hours in the huge gray hall of the Hotel-Hospital, she and Sutton and Gwinnie, while John talked to the President of the Red Cross in his bureau. Everybody looked at them: the door-keeper; the lift-orderly; the ward men and nurses hurrying past; wide stares and sharp glances falling on her and Gwinnie, slanting downwards to their breeches and puttees, then darting upwards to their English faces.

Sutton moved, putting his broad body between them and the batteries of amused and interested eyes.

They stood close together at the foot of the staircase. Above them the gigantic Flora leaned forward, holding out her flowers to preoccupied people who wouldn't look at her; she smiled foolishly; too stupid to know that the Flandria was no longer an hotel but a military hospital.

THE ROMANTIC

John came out of the President's bureau. He looked disgusted and depressed.

'They can put us up,' he said; 'but I've got to break it to you that we're not the only Field Ambulance in Ghent.'

Charlotte said, 'Oh, well, we'd no business to suppose we were.'

'We've got to share our quarters with the other one. . . . It calls itself the McClane Corps.'

'Shall we have to sleep with it?' Sutton said.

'We shall have to have it in our messroom. I believe it's up there now.'

'Well, that won't hurt us.'

'What'll hurt us is this. It'll be sent out before we are. McClane was here hours ago. He's been to headquarters.'

Sutton's gloom deepened. 'How do you know?'

'President says so.'

They went, following the matron, up the gray, tessellated stairs; at each landing the long, gray corridors were tunnels for the passage of strange smells, ether and iodine and carbolic and the faint odour of drains, seeking their outlet at the well of the staircase.

On the third floor, at the turn of the corridor,

a small vestibule between two glass doors led to a room flooded with a blond light from the south. Beyond the glass doors, their figures softened by the deep, doubled shimmer of the panes, they saw the little man in shabby tweeds, the two women, and the seven other men. This, Madame explained, was Dr Donald McClane's Field Ambulance Corps. You could see *it* had thought it was the only one. As they entered they met the swoop of two beautiful, indignant eyes, a slow turning and abrupt stiffening of shoulders; the movement of the group was palpable, a tremor of hostility and resentment.

It lasted with no abatement while Madame, standing there in her gaunt Flemish graciousness, murmured names. 'Mrs Rankin———' Mrs Rankin nodded insolently and turned away. 'Miss Bartrum———' Miss Bartrum, the rather charming one, bowed, drawing the shadow of grave eyebrows over sweet eyes. 'Dr Donald McClane———' As he bowed, the commandant's stare arched up at them, then dropped, suddenly innocent, suddenly indifferent.

They looked round. Madame and her graciousness had gone. Nobody made a place for them at the two long tables set together in the middle

THE ROMANTIC

of the room. The McClane Corps had spread itself over all the chairs and benches, in obstinate possession. They passed out through the open French windows on to the balcony.

It looked south over the railway towards the country where they thought the fighting must be. They could see the lines where the troop trains ran, going north-west and south-east, and the railway station and post office all in one long red-brick building that had a flat roof with a crenellated parapet. Grass grew on the roof. And beyond the black railway lines miles upon miles of flat, open country, green fields, rows of poplars standing up in them very straight; little woods; here and there a low rise bristling and dark with trees. The fighting must be over there. Under the balcony the white street ran south-eastward, and scouting cars and ammunition wagons and long lines of troops were all going that way.

While they talked they remained aware of the others. They could see McClane rubbing his hands; they heard his brief laugh that had no amusement in it, and his voice saying, 'Anyhow, we've got in first.'

When they came back into the room they found the tables drawn apart with a wide space between. The Belgian orderlies were removing plates and cups from one to the other, establishing under the commandant's directions a separate mess. By tea-time two chauffeurs had added themselves to the McClane Corps.

Twelve to four. And they would have to live together, nobody knew how long: as long as the war lasted.

That evening, in the bedroom that John shared with Sutton they sat on two beds, discussing their prospects. Gwinnie was voluble.

'They've driven us out of our messroom with their beastliness. We shall have to sit in our bedrooms all the time.'

'We'd better let the office know we're here,' said Sutton, 'in case we're sent for.'

'Anyhow,' said Charlotte, '*I'm* going to bed.'

John smiled. A struggling, dejected smile.

'My dear child, I've told you they're not going to send us out first.'

'I don't know——' said Gwinnie.

'I *do* know. We shall be lucky if we get a look in when McClane's cars break down.'

'That's it. Have you seen their cars? I

THE ROMANTIC

overhauled them this morning, in the yard. They're nothing but old lorries converted. And one of 'em's got solid tyres.'

'Well?'

'Well—you wait.'

They waited. Even the McClane Corps had to wait.

'I don't care,' said Charlotte, 'how beastly they are to me, provided they leave John alone.'

'What can they do?' he said. 'They don't matter.'

'They're such a lot of them,' said Gwinnie. 'It's when they're all together they're so poisonous.'

'It's when they're *separate*,' Charlotte said. 'I think Mrs Rankin *does* things. And there's McClane swearing he'll get us out of Belgium. But he won't.'

She didn't care. She had got used to it as she had got used to the messroom and its furnishings, the basket-chairs and backless benches, the two long tables covered with white marbled American leather, the photographs of the King and Queen of the Belgians above the chimney piece. The atmosphere of hostility was thick and penetrating, something that you breathed in with the smells of ether and iodine and disinfectant, that hung about the gray, leaking corridors and floated in the blond light of the room. She could feel a secret threat in it, as if at any minute it might work up to some pitch still more malignant, some supreme disaster. There were moments when she wondered whether McClane had prejudiced the authorities against them. At first she had regarded the little man as negligible; it was the women who had fascinated her, as if they had or might come to have for her some profound importance and significance. She didn't like McClane. He straddled too much. But you couldn't go on ignoring him. His dreamy, innocent, full face with its arching eyes, was a mask, the mask of dangerous, inimical intentions; his profile was rough cut, brutal, energetic, you guessed the upper lip thin and hard under the hanging moustache; the lower one stuck out like a sucker. That was his real face. It showed an adhesive, exhausting will that squeezed and sucked till it had got what it wanted out of people. He could work things. So could Mrs Rankin. She had dined with the Colonel.

Charlotte didn't care. She *liked* that beastliness, that hostility of theirs. It was something you could put your back against; it braced her

THE ROMANTIC

to defiance. It brought her closer to John, to John and Gwinnie, and shut them in together more securely. Sutton she was not quite so sure about. Through all their depression he seemed to stand apart somehow by himself in a profounder discontent. 'There are only four of us,' he said; 'we can't call ourselves a corps.' You could see the way his mind was working.

Then suddenly the atmosphere lifted at one point. Mrs Rankin changed her attitude to John. You could see her beautiful hawk's eyes pursuing him about the room. When she found him in the corridors or on the stairs she stopped him and chattered; under her breath because of the hushed wards.

He told Charlotte about it.

'That Mrs Rankin seems inclined to be a bit too friendly.'

'I haven't noticed it.'

'Not with you. With Sutton and—and me.'

'Well——'

'Well, I can't answer for Sutton, but I don't like it. That isn't what we're out here for.'

They were going into the messroom together towards dinner time. Mrs Rankin and Alice Bartrum were there alone, seated at their table, ready. Mrs Rankin called out in her stressed, vibrating voice across the room.

'Mr *Conway*, you people ought to come in with *us*.'

'Why?'

'*Because* there are only four of you and we're twelve. Sixteen's the proper number for a unit. Alice, didn't I say, the minute I saw Mr Conway with that car of his, didn't I say we ought to have him?'

'You did.'

'Thanks. I'd rather take my orders from the Colonel.'

'And *I*'d rather take *mine* from you than from McClane. Fancy coming out at the head of a field ambulance looking like that. Tell you what, Mr Conway, if you'll join up with us I'll get the Colonel to make you our commandant.'

Alice Bartrum opened her shadowed eyes. 'Trixie—you *can't*.'

'Can't I? I can make the old boy do anything I like.'

John stiffened. 'You can't make me do anything you like, Mrs Rankin. You'd much better stick to McClane.'

'What do any of us know about McClane?'

'What do you know about me?'

THE ROMANTIC

You could see how he hated her.

'I know you mean business.'

'Doesn't he?'

'Don't ask me what he *means*.'

She shrugged her shoulders violently. 'Come over here and sit by me. I want to talk to you. Seriously.'

She had shifted her seat and made a place for him beside her on the bench. Her flushed, handsome face covered him with its smile. You could see she was used to being obeyed when she smiled like that; when she sent that light out of her eyes men did what she wanted. All her life the men she knew had obeyed her, all except McClane. She didn't know John.

He raised his head and looked at her with cool, concentrated dislike.

'I'd rather stay where I am if you don't mind. I want to talk to Miss Redhead.'

'Oh——' Mrs Rankin's flush went out like a blown flame. Her lips made one pale, tight thread above the set square of her chin. All her light was in her eyes. They stared before her at the glass door where McClane was entering.

He came swaggering and slipped into his place between her and Alice Bartrum, with his

JOHN RODEN CONWAY

air of not seeing Mrs Rankin, of not seeing Charlotte and John, of not seeing anything he didn't want to see. Presently he bobbed round in his seat so as to see Sutton, and began talking to him excitedly.

At the end of it Charlotte and Sutton found themselves alone, smiling into each other's faces.

'Do you like him?' she said.

'I'm not sure. All the same, that isn't a bad idea of Mrs Rankin's.'

It was Sutton who tried to work it the next morning, sounding McClane.

Charlotte was in the space between the glass doors, arranging their stores in their own cupboard. McClane's stores had overflowed into it on the lower shelves. She could hear the two men talking in the room, Sutton's low, persuasive voice; she couldn't hear what he was saying.

Suddenly McClane brought his fist down on the table.

'I'll take you. And I'll take your women. And I'll take your ambulances. I could do with two more ambulances. But I won't take Conway.'

'You can't tell him that.'

'Can't I?'

THE ROMANTIC

' What can you say ? '

' I can say——— '

She pushed open the glass door and went in. McClane was whispering furtively. She saw Sutton stop him with a look. They turned to her, and Sutton spoke.

' Come in, Miss Redhead. This concerns you. Dr McClane wants you and Miss Denning and me to join his corps.'

' And how about Mr Conway ? '

' Well——— ' McClane was trying to look innocent. ' Mr Conway's just the difficulty. There can't be two commandants in one corps, and he says he won't take orders from me.'

(Mrs Rankin must have talked about it, then.)

' Is that what you told Dr Sutton ? '

' Yes.'

His cold, innocent, blue eyes supported him. He was lying; she knew he was lying; that was not what he had said when he had whispered.

' You don't suppose,' she said, ' I should leave Mr Conway ? And if I stick to him Gwinnie'll stick.'

' And Dr Sutton ? '

' He can please himself.'

' If Miss Redhead stays I shall stay.'

' John will let you off like a shot, if you don't want to.'

She turned to go, and McClane called after her, ' My offer remains open to you three.'

Through the glass door she heard Sutton saying, ' If you're right, McClane, I can't very well leave her with him, can I ? '

Sutton was stupid. He didn't understand. Lying on her bed that night Charlotte made it out.

' Gwinnie—you know why McClane won't have John ? '

' I suppose because Mrs Rankin's keen on him.'

' McClane isn't keen on Mrs Rankin. . . . Can't you see he's trying to hoof John out of Belgium, because he wants all the glory to himself. We wouldn't do that to one of them, even if we were mean enough not to want them in it.'

' He wanted Sutton.'

' Oh, Sutton—he wasn't afraid of *him*. . . . When you think of the war—and think of people being like that. Jealous. Hating each other——'

You mightn't like Mrs Rankin, Mrs Rankin and McClane; but you couldn't say they weren't splendid.

THE ROMANTIC

Five days had passed. On the third day the McClane Corps had been sent out. (Mrs Rankin had not dined with the Colonel for nothing.)

It went again and again. By the fifth day they knew that it had distinguished itself at Alost and Termonde and Quatrecht. The names sounded in their brains like a song with an exciting, maddening refrain. October stretched before them, golden and blank, a volume of tense, vibrating time.

Nothing for it but to wait and wait. The summons might come any minute. Charlotte and Gwinnie had begun by sitting on their driver's seats in the ambulances standing in the yard, ready to start the very instant it came. Their orders were to hold themselves in readiness. They held themselves in readiness and saw McClane's cars swing out from the rubbered sweep in front of the hospital three and four times a day. They stood on their balcony and watched them rush along the road that led to the battlefields south-east of the city. The sight of the flat Flemish land and the sadness of the lovely days oppressed them. She felt that it must be partly that, the incredible loveliness of the days. They sat brooding over the map of Belgium, marking down the names of the places, Alost,

Termonde, and Quatrecht, that McClane had gone to, that he would talk about on his return, when an awful interest would impel them to listen. He and Mrs Rankin would come in about tea-time, swaggering and excited, telling everybody that they had been in the line of fire; and Alice Bartrum would move about the room, quiet and sweet, cutting bread and butter, and pretending to be unconcerned in the narration.

And in the evening, after dinner, the discussions went on and on in John's bedroom. He raged against his infernal luck. If they thought he was going to take it lying down——

'McClane can keep me out of my messroom, but he can't keep me out of my job. There's room in "the line of fire" for both of us.'

'How are we going to get into it?' said Sutton.

'Same way as McClane. If he can go to headquarters, so can I.'

'I wouldn't,' Sutton said. 'It might give a bad impression. Our turn'll come before long.'

Gwinnie laughed. 'It won't—unless Charlotte dines with the Colonel.

'It certainly *mayn't*,' said Charlotte. 'They may commandeer our cars and give them to McClane.'

THE ROMANTIC

'They can't,' said Gwinnie. 'We're volunteers.'

'They can do anything they choose. Military necessity.'

Gwinnie was thoughtful.

'John,' she said, 'can I have one of the cars to-morrow afternoon?'

'What for?'

'Never mind. Can I?'

'You can have both the damned things if you like; they're no good to me.'

The next afternoon they looked on while Gwinnie, who wore a look of great wisdom and mystery, slipped her car out of the yard into a side street and headed for the town. She came back at tea-time, bright-eyed and faintly flushed.

'You'll find we shall be sent out to-morrow.'

'Oh, shall we?' John said.

'Yes. I've worked it for you.'

'You?'

'Me. They've seen my car.'

'Who have?'

'The whole lot of them. General Staff. First of all I paraded it all round the blessed town. Then I turned into the Place d'Armes. I kept it standing two solid hours outside the Hotel de la Poste, where the blooming brass hats all

JOHN RODEN CONWAY

hang out. In five minutes it collected a small crowd. First it was only refugees and war correspondents. Then the Colonel came out and stuck his head in at the back. He got quite excited when he saw we could take five stretcher cases. I showed him our tyres and the electric light, and I ran the stretchers in and out for him. He'd never seen them with wheels before. . . . He said it was *magnifique*. . . . The old bird wanted to take me into the hotel and stand me tea.'

'Didn't you let him?'

'No. I said I had to stay with my car. And I took jolly good care to let him know it hadn't been out yet.'

'Whatever made you think of it?'

'I don't know. It just sort of came to me.'

Next afternoon John had orders to go to Berlaere to fetch wounded.

VIII

At the turn of the road they heard the guns: a solemn Boom—Boom coming up out of hushed spaces; they saw white puffs of smoke rising in the blue sky. The French guns somewhere back of them. The German guns in front, southwards beyond the river.

Charlotte looked at John; he was brilliantly happy. They smiled at each other as if they said, '*Now* it's beginning.'

Outside the village of Berlaere they were held up by two sentries with rifles. (Thrilling, that.) Their Belgian guide leaned out and whispered the password; John showed their passports, and they slipped through.

Where the road turned on their left into the street they saw a group of soldiers standing at the door of a house. Three of them, a Belgian lieutenant and two non-commissioned officers advanced hurriedly and stopped the car. The lieutenant forbade them to go on.

'But,' John said, 'we've got orders to go on.'

JOHN RODEN CONWAY

A shrug intimated that their orders were not the lieutenant's affair. They couldn't go on.

'But we *must* go on. We've got to fetch some wounded.'

'There aren't any wounded,' said the lieutenant.

Charlotte had an inspiration. 'You tell us that tale every time,' she said, 'and there are always wounded.'

The Belgian guide and the lieutenant exchanged glances.

'I've told you there aren't any,' the lieutenant said. 'You must go back.'

'Here—you explain.'

But instead of explaining the little Belgian backed up the lieutenant by a refusal on his own part to go on.

'He can please himself. *We*'re going on.'

'You don't imagine,' Charlotte said, 'by any chance that we're *afraid*?'

The lieutenant smiled, a smile that lifted his ferocious, upturned moustache: first sign that he was yielding. He looked at the sergeant and the corporal, and they nodded.

John had his foot on the clutch. 'We're due,' he said, 'at the dressing-station by three o'clock.'

THE ROMANTIC

She thought: He's magnificent. She could see that the lieutenant and the soldiers thought he was magnificent. Supposing she had come out with some meek fool who would have gone back when they told him——

The lieutenant skipped aside before the advancing car. 'You can go,' he said, 'to the dressing-station.'

'They always do that as a matter of form—sort of warning us that it's our own risk. They won't be responsible.'

She didn't answer. She was thinking that when they turned John's driving place would be towards the German guns.

'I wish you'd let me drive. You know I like driving.'

'Not this time.'

At the dressing-station, a deserted store, they found a Belgian Army Medical officer engaged with a tired and flushed and dirty soldier. He was bandaging his left hand, which had made a trail of blood splashes from the street to the counter. The right hand hung straight down from a nick in the dropped wrist where a tendon had been severed. He told them that they had grasped the situation. Seven men waited there for transport.

JOHN RODEN CONWAY

The best thing—perhaps—he looked doubtfully at Charlotte—would be for them to take these men back at once. (The tired soldier murmured something: a protest or an entreaty.) Though they were not exactly urgent cases. They could wait.

Charlotte suspected a serious reservation. 'You mean you have others more urgent?'

The soldier got in his word. 'Much more.' His lips and eyes moved excitedly in the flush and grime.

'Well, yes,' the doctor admitted that they had. Not in the village, but in a hamlet about a mile outside it. An outpost. This man and three others had been holding it with two machine-guns. He had had a finger shot away and his wrist cut open by a shell-burst; the other three were left there, badly wounded.

'All right, we'll go and fetch them.'

'Monsieur, the place is being shelled. You have no orders.'

'We've no orders not to.'

The doctor spread out helpless palms, palms that disclaimed responsibility.

'If you go, you go at your own risk. I will not send you.'

'That's all right.'

THE ROMANTIC

'Oh, well—but certainly Mademoiselle must be left behind.'

'Mademoiselle is much too useful.'

Frantic gestures of eyebrows and palms.

'You must not stay there more than three minutes. *Three minutes.*'

He turned to the cut tendon with an air of integrity, his conscience appeased by laying down this time limit.

John released the clutch, and the soldier shouted out something, they couldn't make out what, that ended with 'mitrailleuses.'

As they ran down the street the solemn Boom—Boom came right and left; they were now straight between the two batteries.

'Are you all right, Sharlie?'

'Rather.'

The little Belgian by her side muttered, protesting.

'We're not really in any danger. It's all going on over our heads.'

'Do you suppose,' she said, 'they'll get our range?'

'Rather not. Why should they? They've got their range and they'll stick to it.'

The firing on their right ceased.

'They're quiet enough now,' she said.

The little Belgian informed her that if they were quiet so much the worse. They were finding their range.

She thought: We were safe enough before, but———

' Supposing,' she said, ' they alter their range.'

' They won't alter it just for the fun of killing us. They haven't spotted the batteries yet. It's the batteries they're trying for, not the street.'

But the little Belgian went on protesting.

' What's the matter with him ? '

' He's getting a bit jumpy,' she said, ' that's all.'

' Tell him to buck up. Tell him it's all right.'

She translated. The little Belgian shook his head, mournfully persistent. ' Monsieur,' he said, ' didn't know.'

' Oh, yes, he does know.'

It was absurd of the little man to suppose you didn't know, when the noise of the French guns told them how near they were to the enemy's target.

She tried not to listen to him. His mutterings broke up the queer stillness that held her after she had heard the guns. It was only by keeping still that you felt, wave by wave, the rising thrill

THE ROMANTIC

of the adventure. Only by keeping still she was aware of what was passing in John's mind. He knew. He knew. They were one in the almost palpable excitement that they shared; locked close, closer than their bodies could have joined them, in the strange and poignant ecstasy of danger.

There was the sound of an explosion somewhere in front of them beyond the houses.

'Did you hear that, mademoiselle?'

'I did.'

'Miles away,' said John.

She knew it wasn't. She thought: He doesn't want me to know. He thinks I'll be frightened. I mustn't tell him.

But the Belgian had none of John's scruples. The shell was near, he said; very near. It had fallen in the place they were going to.

'But that's the place where the wounded men are.'

He admitted that it was the place where the wounded men were.

They were out of the village now. Their road ran through flat, open country, a causeway raised a little above the level of the fields. No cover anywhere from the fire if it came. The Belgian had begun again.

'What's that he's saying now?'

'He says we shall give away the position of the road.'

'It's the one they told us to take. We've got to go on it. He's in a beastly funk. That's what's the matter with him.'

The Belgian shrugged his shoulders as much as to say he had done his duty and things might now take their course, and they were mistaken if, for one minute, they supposed he was afraid. But they had not gone fifty yards before he begged to be put down. He said it was absolutely necessary that he should go back to the village and collect the wounded there and have them ready for the ambulance on its return.

They let him go. Charlotte looked round the corner of the hood and saw him running with brief, jerky strides.

'He's got a nerve,' said John, 'to be able to do it.'

'What excuse do you think he'll make?'

'Oh, he'll say we sent him.'

The straight dyke of the road went on and on. Seen from the sunk German lines, the heavy ambulance car would look like a house on wheels running along a wall. She thought again

THE ROMANTIC

of John on his exposed seat. If only he had let her drive—but that was absurd. Of course he wouldn't let her. If you were to keep on thinking of the things that might happen to John—— Meanwhile nothing could take from them the delight of this dangerous run across the open. She had to remind herself that the adventure, the romance of it was not what mattered most; it was not the real thing, the thing they had gone out for.

When they came to the wounded, when they came to the wounded, then it would begin.

The hamlet began to show now; it sat on one side of the road, low and alone in the flat land, an open field in front of it, and at the bottom of the field the river and a line of willows, and behind the willows the Germans, hidden. White smoke curled among the branches. You could see it was an outpost, one of the points at which the Germans, if they broke through, would come into the village. They supposed that the house where the wounded men were would be the last of the short row.

Here on their right there were no houses, only the long, high flank of a barn. The parts that had been built out into the field were shelled away, but the outer wall by the roadside still held. It was all that stood between them and the German guns. They drew up the car under its shelter and got down.

They could see all the houses of the hamlet at once on their left; white-washed walls; slender gray doors and shutters. The three that looked out on to the barn were untouched. A few yards ahead a small, empty wine-shop faced the open field; its doorstep and the path in front of its windows glittered with glass dust, with spikes and splinters, and heaped shale of glass that slid and cracked under your feet. Beyond it, a house with its door and all its windows and the front slope of its roof blown in. A broken shutter sagged from the wall. Then the shell of the last house; it pricked up one plastered gable, white and hard against the blue.

They found the men in the last house but one, the house with the broken shutter. They went, carrying their stretchers and the haversack of dressings, under the slanted lintel into the room. The air in there was hot and stifling and thickened with a gray, powdery swarm. Their feet sank through a layer of pinkish, grayish dust.

The three wounded men lay stretched out on this floor, among brickbats and broken panes and slabs of dropped plaster. A thin gray powder

THE ROMANTIC

had settled on them all. And by the side of each man the dust was stiffened into a red cake with a glairy pool in the middle of it, fed from the raw wound; and where two men lay together their pools had joined and overflowed in a thin red stream.

John put down his stretcher and stood still. His face was very white, and his upper lip showed indrawn and dry, and tightened as though it were glued to his teeth.

'John, you *aren't* going to faint, or be sick, or anything?'

'I'm all right.'

He went forward, clenching his fists; moving in a curious, drawn way, like a sleep-walker.

They were kneeling in the dust now, looking for the wounds.

'We must do this chap with the arm first. He'll want a tourniquet.'

He spoke in a husky whisper, as if he were half asleep. . . .

The wounded head stuck to the floor. They scraped round and under it, digging with their hands; it came up wearing a crust of powdered lime. A pad and a bandage. They couldn't do anything more for that. . . . The third man, with the fractured shin-bone and the big flesh wound in his thigh, must have splints and a dressing.

She wondered how John would set about his work. But his queer, hypnotised actions were effectual and clean.

Between them they had fixed the tourniquet.

Through all her preoccupation and the quick, dexterous movements of her hands she could feel her pity tightening her throat: pity that hurt like love, that was delicious and exquisite like love. Nothing mattered, nothing existed in her mind but the three wounded men. John didn't matter. John didn't exist. He was nothing but a pair of hands working quickly and dexterously with her own. . . . She looked up. John's mouth kept its hard, glued look; his eyes were feverish behind a glaze of water, and red-rimmed.

She thought: It's awful for him. He minds too much. It hurt her to see how he minded. After all, he did matter. Deep inside her he mattered more than the wounded men; he mattered more than anything on earth. Only there wasn't time, there wasn't *time* to think of him.

She turned to the next man and caught sight of the two machine guns with their tilted muzzles

THE ROMANTIC

standing in the corner of the room by the chimney. They must remember to bring away the guns.

John's hypnotic whisper came again. 'You might get those splints, Charlotte.'

As she crossed the road a shell fell in the open field beyond, and burst, throwing up a great splash and spray of brown earth. She stiffened herself in an abrupt gesture of defiance. Her mind retorted: 'You've missed, that time. You needn't think I'm going to put myself out for *you*.' To show that she wasn't putting herself out (in case they should be looking) she strolled with dignity to her car, selected carefully the kind of splint she needed, and returned. She thought: Oh, well—supposing they *do* hit. We must get those men out before another comes.

John looked up as she came to him. His face glistened with pinheads of sweat; he panted in the choking air.

'Where did that shell burst?'

'Miles away.'

'Are you certain?'

'Rather.'

She lied. Why not? John had been lying all the time. Lying was part of their defiance, a denial that the enemy's effort had succeeded.

JOHN RODEN CONWAY

Nothing mattered but the fixing of the splints and the carrying of the men. . . .

John was cranking up the engine when she turned back into the house.

'I *say*, what are you doing?'

'Going for the guns.'

There was, she noticed, a certain longish interval between shells. John and the wounded men would be safe from shrapnel under the shelter of the wall. She brought out the first gun and stowed it at the back of the car. Then she went in for the other. It stood on the seat between them with its muzzle pointing down the road. Charlotte put her arm round it to steady it.

On the way back to the dressing-station she sat silent, thinking of the three wounded men in there, behind, rocked and shaken by the jolting of the car on the uneven causeway. John was silent, too, absorbed by his steering.

But as they ran into Ghent the romance of it, the romance of it, came back to her. It wasn't over yet. They would have to go out again for the wounded they had had to leave behind at Berlaere.

'John—John—it's like nothing else on earth.'

'I told you it would be.'

THE ROMANTIC

Slowly realisation came to her. They had brought in their wounded under the enemy's fire. And they had saved the guns.

'Do you mind,' John said, 'if Sutton goes instead of me? He hasn't been out yet?'

'N—no. Not if I can go too.'

'Do you want to?'

'Awfully.'

She had drawn up the ambulance in the square before the hospital and sat in her driver's seat, waiting. Sutton came to her there. When he saw her he stood still.

'*You* going?'

'Rather. Do you mind?'

Sutton didn't answer. All the way out to Berlaere he sat stolid and silent, not looking at anything they passed and taking no more notice of the firing than if he hadn't heard it. As the car swung into Berlaere she was aware of his voice, low under the noise of the engine.

'What did you say?'

'Conway told me it was you who saved the guns.'

Suddenly she was humbled.

'It was the men who saved them. We just brought them away.'

JOHN RODEN CONWAY

'Conway told me what you did,' he said quietly.

Going out with Sutton was a quiet affair.

'You know,' he said presently, 'it was against the Hague Convention.'

'Good Heavens, so it was. I never thought of it.'

'You must think of it. You gave the Germans the right to fire on all our ambulances. . . . You see, this isn't just a romantic adventure, it's a disagreeable, necessary, rather dangerous job.'

'I didn't do it for swank. I knew the guns were wanted, and I couldn't bear to leave them.'

'I know. It would have been splendid if you'd been a combatant. But,' he said sadly, 'this is a field ambulance, not an armoured car.'

IX

She was glad they had been sent out with the McClane Corps to Melle. She wanted McClane to see the stuff that John was made of. She knew what had been going on in the commandant's mind. He had been trying to persuade himself that John was no good, because, from the minute he had seen him with his ambulance on the wharf at Ostend, from the minute he had known his destination, he had been jealous of him and afraid. Why, he must have raced them all the way from Ostend, to get in first. Afraid and jealous, afraid of John's youth with its secret of triumph and of courage; jealous of John's face and body that men and women turned back to look at as they passed; even the soldiers going up to the battlefields, going up to wounds and death, turned to look at this creature of superb and brilliant life. Even on the boat he must have had a dreadful wonder whether John was bound for Ghent; he must have known from the beginning that wherever Conway placed himself he would stand out and make other men look small and insignificant. If he wasn't jealous and afraid of Sutton she supposed it was because John had had that rather diminishing effect on poor Billy.

If Billy Sutton distinguished himself that would open McClane's eyes a little wider, too.

She wondered why Billy kept on saying that McClane was a great psychologist. If it was true that would be very awful for McClane; he would see everything going on inside people, then, all the things he didn't want to see; he wouldn't miss anything, and he would know all the time what John was like. The little man was wilfully shutting his eyes because he was so mean that he couldn't bear to see John as he really was. Now he would have to see.

The thought of McClane's illumination consoled her for her own inferior place in the adventure. This time the chauffeurs would have to stay at the end of the village with their cars. The three were drawn up at the street side, close under the house walls, McClane's first. Then Sutton's, with Gwinnie. Then hers; behind it the short, straight road where the firing would come down.

THE ROMANTIC

John stood in the roadway waiting for the others. He had his hand beside her hand, grasping the arm of the driver's seat.

'I wish you could take me with you,' she said.

'Can't. The orders are, all chauffeurs to stand by the cars.'

. . . His eyebrows knotted and twitched in sudden anxiety.

'You know, Sharlie, you'll be fired on.'

'I know. I don't mind, John, I don't really. I shall be all right.'

'Yes. You'll be all right.' But by the way he kept on glancing up and down the road she could see he was uneasy. 'If you could have stood in front of those cars. *You*'re in the most dangerous place here.'

'Somebody's got to be in it.'

He looked at her and smiled. 'Jeanne,' he said, 'in her armour.'

'Rot.'

And they were silent.

'I say, John—my car *does* cover Gwinnie's a bit, doesn't it?'

'Yes,' he said abruptly.

'*That's* all right. You must go now. They're coming for the stretchers.'

JOHN RODEN CONWAY

His face quivered. He thrust out his hand quickly, and as she took it she thought: He thinks he isn't coming back. She was aware of Mrs Rankin and two of the McClane men with stretchers, passing; she could see Mrs Rankin looking at them as she came on, smiling over her shoulder, drawing the men's attention to their leave-taking.

She thought: *They* don't shake hands when they're going out. They don't think whether they're coming back or not. . . . They don't think at all. But then, none of them were lovers as she and John were lovers.

' John, you'd better go and carry Mrs Rankin's stretcher for her.'

He went.

She watched them as they walked together up the short straight road to the battlefield at the top. Sutton followed with Alice Bartrum; then the McClane men; they nodded to her and smiled. Then McClane, late, running, trying to overtake John and Mrs Rankin, to get to the head of his unit. Perhaps he was afraid that John, in his khaki, would be mistaken for the commandant.

How childish he was with his fear and jealousy. Childish. She thought of his petulant refusal

THE ROMANTIC

to let John come in with them. As if he could really keep him out. When it came to action they *were* one corps; they couldn't very well be divided, since McClane had more men than stretchers and John had more stretchers than men. They would all be infinitely happier, working together like that, instead of standing stupidly apart, glaring and hating.

Yet she knew what McClane and Mrs Rankin had been playing for. McClane, if he could, would have taken their fine Roden cars from them; he would have taken Sutton. She knew that Mrs Rankin would have taken John from her, Charlotte Redhead, if she could.

And when she thought of the beautiful, arrogant woman, marching up to the battlefield with John, she wondered whether, after all, she didn't hate her. . . . No. No. It was horrible to hate a woman who at any minute might be killed. They said McClane didn't look after his women. He didn't care how they exposed themselves to the firing; he took them into unnecessary danger. He didn't care. He was utterly cold, utterly indifferent to everybody and everything except his work of getting in the wounded. . . . Well, perhaps, if he had been decent to John, she wouldn't have believed a

JOHN RODEN CONWAY

word of it, and anyhow they hadn't come out there to be protected.

She had a vision of John and McClane carrying Mrs Rankin between them on a stretcher. That was what would happen if you hated. Hate could kill.

Then John and she were safe. They were lovers. Lovers. Neither of them had ever said the word, but they owned the wonderful, immaterial fact in secret to each other; the thought of it moved in secret behind all their other thoughts. From the moment, just passed, when they held each other's hands she knew that John loved her, not in a dream, not in coldness, but with a queer, unearthly ardour. He had her in his incredible, immaterial way, a way that none of them would understand.

From the Barrow Hill Farm time? Or from yesterday? She didn't know. Perhaps it had gone on all the time; but it would be only since yesterday that he really knew it.

A line of soldiers marched by, going up to the battlefield. They looked at her and smiled, a flashing of bright eyes and teeth all down the line. When they had passed the street was deserted.

. . . That rattle on the stones was the firing.

THE ROMANTIC

It had come at last. She saw Gwinnie looking back round the corner of the hood to see what it was like. She called to her, 'Don't stick your head out, you silly cuckoo. You'll be hit.' She said to herself: If I think about it I shall feel quite jumpy. It was one thing to go tearing along between two booming batteries, in excitement, with an end in view, and quite another thing to sit tight and still on a motionless car, to be fired on. A bit trying to the nerves, she thought, if it went on long. She was glad that her car stood next to the line of fire, sheltering Gwinnie's, and she wondered how John was getting on up there.

The hands of the ambulance clock pointed to half-past three. They had been waiting forty minutes then. She got down to see if any of the stretcher-bearers were in sight.

They were coming back. Straggling, lurching forms. White bandages. The wounded who could walk came first. Then the stretchers.

Alice Bartrum stopped as she passed Charlotte. The red had gone from her sunburn, but her face was undisturbed.

'You've got to wait here,' she said, 'for Mr Conway and Sutty. And Trixie and Mac.

JOHN RODEN CONWAY

They mayn't be back for ages. They've gone miles up the field.'

She waited.

The front cars had been loaded, had driven off and returned three times. It was six o'clock before John appeared with Mrs Rankin.

She heard Mrs Rankin calling sharply to her to get down and give a hand with the stretcher.

John and Mrs Rankin were disputing.

'*Can't* you shove it in at the bottom?' he was saying.

'*No.* The first cases *must* go on top.'

Her mouth snapped like a clamp. Her eyes were blazing. She was struggling with the head of the stretcher while John heaved at the foot. He staggered as he moved, and his face was sallow-white and drawn and glistening. When Charlotte took the shafts from him they were slippery with his sweat.

'Is he hurt?' she whispered.

'Very badly hurt,' said Mrs Rankin.

'John, I mean.'

Mrs Rankin snorted. 'You'd better ask him.'

John was slouching round to the front of the car, anxious to get out of the sight and sound of

THE ROMANTIC

her. He went with an uneven dropping movement of one hip. Charlotte followed him.

'Get into your seat, Sharlie. We've got to wait for Billy and McClane.'

He dragged himself awkwardly into the place beside her.

'John,' she said, 'are you hurt?'

'No. But I think I've strained something. That's why I couldn't lift that damned stretcher.'

The windows stood wide open to the sweet, sharp air. She heard Mrs Rankin and Sutton talking on the balcony. In that dreadful mess-room you heard everything.

'What do you suppose it was then?' Mrs Rankin said.

And Sutton, 'Oh, I don't know. Something upset him.'

'If he's going to be upset *like that* every time, he'd better go home.'

They were talking—she knew they were talking about John.

'Hallo, Charlotte, we haven't left you much tea.'

'It doesn't matter.'

Her hunger left her suddenly. She stared

with disgust at the remains of the tea the McClane Corps had eaten.

Sutton went on. 'He hasn't been sleeping properly. I've made him go to bed.'

'If you can keep him in bed for the duration of the war——'

'Are you talking about John?'

'We are.'

'I don't know what you're driving at; but I suppose he was sick on that beastly battlefield. It's all very well for you two; you're a trained nurse and Billy's a surgeon. . . . You aren't taken that way when you see blood.'

'Blood?' said Mrs Rankin.

'Yes. Blood. He was perfectly all right yesterday.'

Mrs Rankin laughed. 'Yesterday he couldn't see there was any danger. You could tell that by the idiotic things he said.'

'I saw it. And if I could he could.'

'Funny kid. You'd better get on with your tea. You'll be sent out again before you know where you are.'

Charlotte settled down. Sutton was standing beside her now, cutting bread and butter.

'Hold on,' he said. 'That tea's all stewed and cold. I'll make you some of mine.'

THE ROMANTIC

She drank the hot, fragrant China tea he brought her.

Presently she stood up. 'I think I'll take John some of this.'

'Best thing you can give him,' Sutton said. He got up and opened the doors for her, the glass doors and the door of the bedroom.

She sat down beside John's bed and watched him while he drank Sutton's tea. He said he was all right now. No. He hadn't ruptured anything; he only thought he had; but Sutton had overhauled him and said he was all right.

And all the time his face was still vexed and drawn. Something must have happened out there; something that hurt him to think of.

'John,' she said, 'I wish I'd gone with you instead of Mrs Rankin.'

'I wish to God you had. Everything's all right when you're with me, and everything's all wrong when you're not.'

'How do you mean, wrong?'

He shook his head, frowning slightly, as a sign for her to stop. Sutton had come into the room.

'You needn't go,' he said. 'I've only come for my coat and my case. I've got to help with the operations.'

JOHN RODEN CONWAY

He slipped into his white linen coat. There were thin smears of blood on the sleeves and breast. He groped about the room, peering short-sightedly for his case of instruments.

'John, was Mrs Rankin any good?' she asked presently.

John lay back and closed his eyes as if to shut out the sight of Mrs Rankin.

'Don't talk to me,' he said, 'about that horrible woman.'

Sutton had turned abruptly from his search. 'Good?' he said. 'She was magnificent. So was Miss Bartrum. So was McClane.'

John opened his eyes. 'So was Charlotte.'

'I quite agree with you.' Sutton had found his case. His face was hidden by the raised lid as he peered, examining his instruments. He spoke abstractedly. 'Magnificent.'

When he left the room Charlotte followed him.

'Billy——'

'Well——'

He stopped in his noiseless course down the corridor.

'What was it?' she said. 'What happened?'

He didn't pretend not to understand her.

'Oh, nothing. Conway and Mrs Rankin didn't hit it off very well together.'

THE ROMANTIC

They spoke in low, rapid tones, conscious always of the wards behind the shut doors. Her feet went fast and noiseless beside his as he hurried to the operating theatre. They came out on to the wide landing and waited there by the brass lattice of the lift.

'How do you mean, hit it off?'

'Oh, well, she thought he didn't come up quick enough with a stretcher, and she pitched into him.'

'But he was dead beat. Done. Couldn't she see that?'

'No. I don't suppose she could. She was a bit excited.'

'She was horrible.' Now that Mrs Rankin was back safe she hated her. She knew she hated her.

'A bit cruel, perhaps. All the same,' he said, 'she was magnif——'

The lift had come hissing and wailing up behind him. The orderly stood in it, staring at Sutton's back, obsequious, yet impatient. She thought of the wounded men in the theatre downstairs.

'You mustn't keep them waiting,' she said.

He stepped back into the lift. It lowered him rapidly. His chin was on a level with the floor when his mouth tried again and succeeded: 'Magnificent.'

And she knew that she had followed him out to hear him say that John had been magnificent too.

Gwinnie was looking in at the messroom door and saying, 'Do you know where Charlotte is?' Mrs Rankin's voice called out, 'I think you'll find her in *Mr Conway*'s bedroom.' One of the chauffeurs laughed. Charlotte knew what they were thinking.

Gwinnie failed to retort. She was excited, shaken out of her stolidity.

'Oh, there you are! I've got something ripping to tell you. Not in here.'

They slouched, with their arms slung affectionately round each other's waists, into their own room. Behind the shut door Gwinnie began.

'The Colonel's most frightfully pleased about Berlaere.'

'Does he think they'll hold it?'

'It isn't that. He's pleased about you.'

'Me?'

'You and John. What you did there. And your bringing back the guns.'

'Who told you that?'

THE ROMANTIC

'Mac. The old boy was going on to him like anything about you last night. It means you'll be sent out every time. Every time there's anything big on.'

'Oh-h! Let's go and tell John. . . . I suppose,' she added, 'that's what was the matter with Mrs Rankin.'

She wondered whether it had been the matter with Billy Sutton too; if he too were jealous and afraid.

That night Mrs Rankin told her what the Colonel really had said: '" C'est magnifique, mais ce n'est pas—la Croix Rouge." If you're all sent home to-morrow it'll serve you jolly well right,' she said.

But somehow she couldn't make it sound as if he had been angry.

X

SHE waited.

John had told her to stay there with the wounded man up the turn of the stable yard while he went for the stretcher. His car, packed with wounded, stood a little way up the street, headed for Ghent. Sutton's car, with one of McClane's chauffeurs, was in front of it, ready; she could hear the engine purring.

Instead of going at once for the stretcher John had followed Sutton into the house opposite, the house with the narrow gray shutters. And he had called to her again across the road to wait for him.

Behind her in the yard the wounded man sat on the cobble-stones, his back propped against the stable wall. He was safe there, safer than he would have been outside in the ambulance.

It was awful to think that he would have been left behind if they had not found him at the last minute among the straw.

THE ROMANTIC

She went and stood by the yard entrance to see whether John were coming with the stretcher. A soldier came out of the house with the narrow shutters, wounded, limping, his foot bound to a splint. Then Sutton came, hurrying to help him. He shouted to her, 'Come on, Charlotte, hurry up!' and she called back, 'I've got to wait here for John.'

She watched them go on slowly up the road to Sutton's car; she saw them get in; she saw the car draw out and rush away.

Then she saw John come out to the door of the house and stand there, looking up and down the street. Once she saw him glance back over his shoulder at something behind him in the room. The same instant she heard the explosion and saw the shell burst in the middle of the street, not fifty yards from the ambulance. Half a minute after she saw John dash from the doorway and run, run at an incredible pace, towards his car. She heard him crank up the engine.

She supposed that he was going to back towards the yard, and she wondered whether she could lift up the Belgian and carry him out. She stooped over him, put her hands under his armpits, raising him and wondering. Better not.

JOHN RODEN CONWAY

He had a bad wound. Better wait for the stretcher.

She turned, suddenly arrested. The noise she heard was not the grating noise of a car backing, it was the scream of a car getting away; it dropped to a heavy whirr and diminished.

She looked out. Up the road she saw John's car rushing furiously towards Ghent.

The Belgian had heard it. His eyes moved. Black, hare's eyes, terrified. It was not possible, he said, that they had been left behind?

No, it was not possible. John had forgotten them; but he would remember; he would come back. In five minutes. Seven minutes. She had waited fifteen.

The Belgian was muttering something. He complained of being left there. He said he was not anxious about himself, but about mademoiselle. Mademoiselle ought not to have been left. She was sitting on the ground now, beside him.

'It'll be all right,' she said. 'He'll come back.' When he remembered he would come back.

She had waited half an hour.

Another shell. It had burst over there at the backs of the houses, beyond the stable.

THE ROMANTIC

She wondered whether it would be safer to drag her man across the street under the wall of the Town Hall. They would be sure to aim at it and miss it, whereas any minute they might hit the stable.

At the moment while she wondered there was a third tremendous explosion, the crash and roar of brickwork, falling like coal down an enormous shute. It came from the other side of the street a little way down. It couldn't be far from the Town Hall. That settled it. Much better stay where they were. The Belgian had put his arm round her, drawing her to him, away from the noise and shock of the shell.

It was clear now that John was not coming back. He had forgotten them.

The Belgian's hold slackened; he dozed, falling against her and recovering himself with a jerk and begging her pardon. She drew down his head on to her shoulder and let it rest there. Her mind was soaked in the smell of his rank breath, of the warm sweat that oozed through his tunic, the hot, fetid smell that came through his unlaced boots. She didn't care; she was too sorry for him. She could feel nothing but the helpless pressure of his body against hers, nothing but her pity that hurt her and was exquisite like love. Yesterday she had thought it would be good to die with John. Now she thought it would be good to die with the wounded Belgian, since John had left her there to die. And again, she had a vehement desire for life, a horror of the unjust death John was bringing on them.

But of course there wouldn't be any death. If nobody came she would walk back to Ghent and bring out the ambulance.

If only he had shouted to her to carry the wounded man and come. In the minute between the concussion of the shell and the cranking of the engine. But she could see him rushing. If only she knew *why* he had left them. . . . She wanted to get back to Ghent, to see John, to know. To know if John—if John really *was*—nothing could be worse than not knowing.

It didn't matter so much about his forgetting her. The awful thing was his forgetting the wounded man. How could you forget a wounded man? When she remembered the Belgian's terrified hare's eyes she hated John.

And, as she sat there supporting his head with her shoulder, she thought again. There must have been a wounded man in the house John had come out of. Was it possible that he had forgotten him, too? ... He hadn't forgotten. She could see him looking back over his shoulder; looking at something that was lying there, that couldn't be anything but a wounded man. Or a dead man. Whatever it was, it had been the last thing he had seen; the last thing he had thought of before he made his dash. It wasn't possible that he had left a wounded man in there, alive. It was not possible.

And all the time, while she kept on telling herself that it was not possible she saw a wounded man in the room John had left; she saw his head turning to the doorway, and his eyes, frightened; she felt his anguish in the moment that he knew himself abandoned. Not forgotten. Abandoned.

She would have to go over to the house and see. She must know whether the man was there or not there. She raised the Belgian's head, gently, from her shoulder. She would have to wake him and tell him what she was going to do, so that he mightn't think she had left him and be frightened.

But the Belgian roused himself to a sudden virile determination. Mademoiselle must *not* cross the road. It was too dangerous.

JOHN RODEN CONWAY

Mademoiselle would be hit. He played on her pity with an innocent, cunning cajolery. 'Mademoiselle must not leave me. I do not want to be left.'

'Only for one minute. One little minute. I think there's a wounded man, like you, monsieur, in that house.'

'Ah-h—a wounded man?' He seemed to acknowledge the integrity of her purpose. 'If only I were not wounded, if only I could crawl an inch, I would go instead of mademoiselle.'

The wounded man lay on the floor of the room in his corner by the fireplace where John had left him. His coat was rolled up under his head for a pillow. He lay on his side, with humped hips and knees drawn up, and one hand, half clenched, half relaxed, on his breast under the drooped chin; so that at first she thought he was alive, sleeping. She knelt down beside him and clasped his wrist; she unbuttoned his tunic and put in her hand under his shirt above the point of his heart. He was certainly dead. No pulse; no beat; no sign of breathing. Yet his body was warm still, and limp as if with sleep. He couldn't have been dead very long.

THE ROMANTIC

And he was young. A boy. Not more than sixteen. John couldn't have left him.

She wasn't certain. She was no nearer certainty so long as she didn't know when the boy had died. If only she knew——

They hadn't unfastened his tunic and shirt to feel over his heart if he were dead. So he couldn't have been dead when they left him. . . . But there was Sutton. Billy wouldn't have left him unless he had been dead. Her mind worked rapidly, jumping from point to point, trying to find some endurable resting place. . . . He was so young, so small, so light. Light. It wouldn't take two to carry him. She could have picked him up and carried him herself. Billy had had the lame man to look after. He had left the boy to John. She saw John looking back over his shoulder.

She got up and went through the house, through all the rooms, to see if there were any more of them that John had left there. She felt tired out and weak, sick with her belief, her fear of what John had done. The dead boy was alone in the house. She covered his face with her handkerchief and went back.

The Belgian waited for her at the entrance to the yard. He had dragged himself there, crawling on his hands and knees. He smiled when he saw her.

'I was coming to look for you, mademoiselle.'

She had him safe beside her against the stable wall. He let his head rest on her shoulder now, glad of the protecting contact. She tried not to think about John. Something closed down between them. Black. Black; shutting him off, closing her heart against him, leaving her heart hard and sick. The light went slowly out of the street, out of the sky. The dark came, the dark sounding with the 'Boom—Boom' of the guns, lit with spiked diamond flashes like falling stars.

The Belgian had gone to sleep again when she heard the ambulance coming down the street.

'Is that you, Charlotte?'
'Billy——! What made you come?'
'Conway. He's in a frantic funk. Said he'd lost you. He thought you'd gone on with me.'

How awful it would be if Billy knew.

'It was my fault,' she lied. 'He told me to go on with you.' She could hear him telling her to wait for him in the stable yard.

THE ROMANTIC

'I'd have come before only I didn't see him soon enough. I had an operation. . . . Is that a wounded man you've got there? I suppose he lost him, too?'

'He didn't know he was here.'

'I see.'

Then she remembered. Billy would know. Billy would tell her.

'Billy—was that boy dead when you left him? The boy in the house over there.'

He was stooping to the Belgian, examining his bandages, and he didn't answer all at once. He seemed to be meditating.

'*Was* he?' she repeated.

It struck her that Billy was surprised.

'Because——' She stopped there. She couldn't say to him, 'I want to know whether John left him dead or alive.'

'He was dead all right.' Sutton's voice came up slow and muffled out of his meditation.

It was all right. She might have known. She might have known. Vaguely for a moment she wondered why Billy had come for her and not John; then she was frightened.

'Billy—John isn't hurt, is he?'

'No. Rather not. A bit done up. I made

JOHN RODEN CONWAY

him go and lie down. . . . Look here, we must get out of this.'

The McClane Corps were gathered on their side of the messroom. They greeted her with shouts of joy, but their eyes looked at her queerly, as if they knew something dreadful had happened to her.

'You should have stood in with us, Charlotte,' Mrs Rankin was saying. 'Then you wouldn't get mislaid among the shells.' She was whispering. 'Dr McClane, if you took Charlotte out among the shells, would you run away and leave her there?'

'I'd try not to.'

Oh, yes. He wouldn't run away and leave her. But he wouldn't care where he took her. He wouldn't care whether a shell got her or not. But John cared. If only she knew *why* . . . Their queer faces sobered her and suddenly she knew. She saw Sutton coming out of the house with the narrow shutters; she heard him shouting to her, 'Come on, Charlotte, hurry up!'

John must have heard him. He must really have thought that she had gone with him.

THE ROMANTIC

But he must have known, too, that she wouldn't go. He must have known that if he told her to wait for him she would wait. So that——

The voices of the McClane women ceased abruptly. One of them turned round. Charlotte saw John standing between the glasses of the two doors. He came in, and she heard Mrs Rankin calling out in her hard, insolent voice, 'Well, Mr Conway, so you've got in safe.'

She was always like that, hard and insolent, with her damned courage. As if courage were ever anything more than just being decent, and as if other people couldn't be decent too. She hated John because she couldn't make him come to her, couldn't make him look with pleasure at her beautiful, arrogant face. She disliked Sutton and McClane for the same reason, but she hated John. He treated her face with a hardness and insolence like her own. You could see her waiting for her revenge, watching every minute for a chance to stick her blade into him. He was pretending that he hadn't heard her.

His hair stood up in pointed tufts, rumpled from his pillow. His eyes had a dazed, stupid look, as if he were not perfectly awake. But at the sound of the rasping voice his mouth had tightened; it was pinched and sharp with pain.

JOHN RODEN CONWAY

He didn't look at Mrs Rankin. He came to her, Charlotte Redhead, straight; straight as if she had drawn him from his sleep.

The McClane people got up, one after another, and went out.

'Charlotte,' he said, 'did you really think I'd left you?'

'I thought you'd left me. But I knew you hadn't.'

'You *knew* it wasn't possible?'

'Yes. Inside me I knew.'

'I'm awfully sorry. Sutton told me you were going on with him, and I thought you'd gone.'

XI

SHE would remember for ever the talk they had on the balcony that day while Antwerp was falling.

They were standing there, she and John Conway and Sutton, looking over the station and the railway lines to the open country beyond: the fields, the tall slender trees, the low mounds of the little hills, bristling and dark. Round the corner of the balcony they could see into the *Place* below; it was filled with a thick, black crowd of refugees. Antwerp was falling.

Presently the ambulance train would come in and they would have to go over there to the station with their stretchers and carry out the wounded. Meanwhile they waited.

John brooded. His face was heavy and sombre with discontent. 'No,' he said. 'No. It isn't good enough.'

'What isn't?'

'What we're doing here. Going to all those little tinpot places. The real fighting isn't down there. They ought to send us to Antwerp.'

'I suppose they send us where they think we're most wanted.'

'I don't believe they do. We were fools not to have insisted on going to Antwerp, instead of letting ourselves be stuck here in a rotten side show.'

'We've had enough to do, anyhow,' said Sutton.

'And there isn't anybody but us and Mac to do it,' Charlotte said.

John's eyebrows twisted. 'Yes; but we're not *in* it. I want to be in it. In the big thing; the big, dangerous thing.'

Sutton sighed and got up and left them. John waited for the closing of the door.

'Does it strike you,' he said, 'that Billy isn't very keen?'

'No. It doesn't. What do you mean?'

'I notice that he's jolly glad when he can get an indoor job.'

'That's because they're short of surgeons. He only wants to do what's most useful.'

'I didn't say he had cold feet.'

'Of course he hasn't. Billy would go to Antwerp like a shot if they'd let him. He feels just as we do about it. That's why he got up and went away.'

'He'd go. But he wouldn't enjoy it.'

'Oh, don't talk about " enjoying." '

'Sharlie, you don't mean to say *you*'re not keen?'

'No. It's only that I don't care as much as I did about what you call the romance of it; and I do care more about the solid work. It seems to me it doesn't matter who does it so long as it's done.'

'I'd very much rather I did it than McClane. So would you.'

'Yes. I would. But I'd be sorry if poor little Mac didn't get any of it. And all the time I know it doesn't matter which of us it is. It doesn't matter whether we're in danger or out of danger, or whether we're in the big thing or a little one.'

'Don't you want to be in the big thing?'

'Yes. I *want*. But I know my wanting doesn't matter. I don't matter. None of us matters.'

That was how she felt about it now that it had come to defeat, now that Antwerp was falling. Yesterday they, she and John, had been vivid entities, intensely real, living and moving in the war as in a containing space that was real enough, since it was there, but real like hell or heaven or God, not to be grasped or felt in its reality; only the stretch of it that they covered was real, the roads round Ghent, the burning villages, the places where they served, Berlaere and Melle, Quatrecht and Zele; the wounded men. Yesterday her thoughts about John had mattered, her doubt and fear of him and her pain; her agony of desire that he should be, should be always, what she loved him for being; and her final certainty had been the one important, the one real thing. To-day she had difficulty in remembering all that, as if *they* hadn't really been. To-day they were unimportant to themselves and to each other; small, not quite real existences enveloped by an immense reality that closed in on them; alive; black, palpitating defeat. It made nothing of them, of their bodies nothing but the parts they worked with: feet and hands. Nothing mattered, nothing existed but the war, and the armies, the Belgian Army, beaten.

Antwerp was falling. And afterwards it would be Ghent, and then Ostend. And then there would be no more Belgium.

But John wouldn't hear of it. Ghent wouldn't fall.

THE ROMANTIC

'It won't fall because it isn't a fortified city,' she objected. 'But it'll surrender. It'll have to.'

'It won't. If the Germans come anywhere near we shall drive them back.'

'They *are* near. They're all round in a ring with only a little narrow opening up *there*. And the ring's getting closer.'

'It's easier to push back a narrow ring than a wide one.'

'It's easier to break through a thin ring than a thick one, and who's going to push?'

'We are. The British. We'll come pouring in, hundreds of thousands of us, through that little narrow opening up there.'

'If we only would——'

'Of course we shall. If I thought we wouldn't, if I thought we were going to let the Belgians down, if we *betrayed* them—my God! I'd kill myself. . . . No. No, I wouldn't. That wouldn't hurt enough. I'd give up my damned country and be a naturalised Belgian. Why, they *trust* us. They trust us to save Antwerp.'

'If we don't, that wouldn't be betrayal.'

'It would. The worst kind. It would be like betraying a wounded man; or a woman. Like me betraying you, Jeanne. You needn't look like that. It's so bad that it can't happen.'

Through the enveloping sadness she felt a prick of joy, seeing him so valiant, so unbeaten in his soul. It supported her certainty. His soul was so big that nothing could satisfy it but the big thing, the big, dangerous thing. He wouldn't even believe that Antwerp was falling.

She knew. She knew. There was not the smallest doubt about it any more. She saw it happen.

It happened in the village near Lokeren, the village whose name she couldn't remember. The Germans had taken Lokeren that morning; they were *in* Lokeren. At any minute they might be in the village.

You had to pass through a little town to get to it. And there they had been told that they must not go on. And they had gone on. And in the village they were told that they must go back and they had not gone back. They had been given five minutes to get in their wounded and they had been there three quarters of an hour, she and John working together, and Trixie Rankin with McClane and two of his men.

Charlotte had been sorry for Sutton and

THE ROMANTIC

Gwinnie and the rest of McClane's Corps who had not come out with them to this new place, but had been sent back again to Melle where things had been so quiet all morning that they hadn't filled their ambulances, and half of them had hung about doing nothing. She had fretted at the stupidity which had sent them where they were not wanted. But here there were not enough hands for the stretchers, and Charlotte was wanted every second of the time. From the first minute you could see what you were in for.

The retreat.

And for an instant, in the blind rush and confusion of it, she had lost sight of John. She had turned the car round and left it with its nose pointing towards Ghent. Trixie Rankin and the McClane men were at the front cars taking out the stretchers; John and McClane were going up the road. She had got out her own stretcher and was following them when the battery came tearing down the road and cut them off. It tore headlong, swerving and careening with great rattling and crashing noises. She could see the faces of the men, thrown back, swaying; there was no terror in them, only a sort of sullen anger and resentment.

JOHN RODEN CONWAY

She stood on the narrow, sandy track beside the causeway to let it pass, and when a gap came in the train she dashed through to get to John. And John was not there. When all the artillery had passed he was not there; only McClane, going on up the middle of the street by himself.

She ran after him and asked him what had happened to John. He turned, dreamy and deliberate, utterly unperturbed. John, he said, had gone on to look for a wounded man who was said to have been taken into one of those houses there, on the right, in the lane. She went down the lane with her stretcher and McClane waited for them at the top. The doors of the houses were open; Flemish women stood outside, looking up to the street. There was one house with a shut door, a tall green door; she thought that would be the one that John had gone into. She rapped, and he opened the door and came striding out, holding his head high. He shut the door quietly and looked at her, an odd look, piercing and grave.

'Dead,' he said.

And when McClane met them he said it again, 'Dead.'

The wounded were being brought down from

THE ROMANTIC

Lokeren in trams that ran on to a siding behind a little fir plantation outside the village. At the wide top of the street a table of boards and trestles stood by the foot track, and the stretchers were laid on it as they came in, and the wounded had their first bandaging and dressings there. McClane took up his place by this table, and the stretcher-bearers went backwards and forwards between the village and the plantation.

Beyond the plantation the flagged road stretched flat and gray, then bent in a deep curve, and on the wider sweep of the curve a row of tall, slender trees stood up like a screen.

It would be round the turn of the road under the trees that the Germans would come when they came. You couldn't lose this sense of them, coming on behind there, not yet seen, but behind, coming on, pursuing the retreat of the batteries. Every now and then they found themselves looking up towards the turn. The gray, bending sweep and the screen of tall trees had a fascination for them, a glamour; and above the movements of their hands and feet their minds watched, intent, excited, but without fear. There was no fear in the village. The women came out of their houses carrying cups of water for the men's thirst; they seemed to be concerned, not

JOHN RODEN CONWAY

with the coming of the Germans, but with the bringing in of the wounded and the presence of the English ambulance in their street.

And the four stretcher-bearers came and went, from house to house and between the village and the plantation, working, working steadily. Yet they were aware all the time of the pursuing terror, behind the turn of the road; they were held still in their intentness. Over all of them was a quiet, fixed serenity. McClane's body had lost its eager, bustling energy and was still; his face was grave, preoccupied and still; only Trixie Rankin went rushing, and calling out to her quiet man in a fierce, dominating excitement.

And in John's face and in his alert body there was happiness, happiness that was almost ecstasy; it ran through and shone from him, firm and still, like a flame that couldn't go out. It penetrated her and made her happy and satisfied and sure of him. She had seen it leap up in him as he swung himself into the seat beside her when they started. He was restless, restless every day until they were sent out; he couldn't wait in peace before they had set off on the adventure, as if he were afraid that at the last minute something would happen to dash his chance from

THE ROMANTIC

him. She couldn't find this passionate uneasiness in herself; she waited with a stolid trust in the event; but she had something of his feeling. After all, it was there, the romance, the fascination, the glamour; you couldn't deny it any more than you could deny the beating of the blood in your veins. It was their life.

They had been in the village three-quarters of an hour. John and Charlotte waited while McClane at his table was putting the last bandage on the last wound. In another minute they would be gone. It was then that the Belgian Red Cross man came running to them. Had they taken a man with a wound in his back? A bad wound? As big as that? No? Then he was still here, and he had got to take him to the ambulance. No, he didn't know where he was. He might be in one of those houses where they took in the wounded, or he might be up there by the tramway in the plantation. Would they take a stretcher and find him? *He* had to go back to the tramway. The last tram was coming in from Lokeren. He ran back, fussy and a little frightened.

John shouted out, 'Hold on, McClane, there's another tram coming,' and set off up the street. They had taken all the men out of the houses;

therefore the man with the bad wound must have been left somewhere by the plantation. They went there, carrying their stretcher, going, going up to the last minute, in delight, in the undying thrill of the danger.

The wounded man was not in the plantation. As they looked 'for him the tram from Lokeren slid in, Red Cross men on the steps, clinging. The doors were flung open and the wounded men came out, stumbling, falling, pushing each other. Somebody cried, 'No stretchers! Damned bad management. With the Germans on our backs.' A Red Cross man, with a puffed white face, stood staring at John and Charlotte, stupefied.

'Are they coming?' John said.

'Coming? They'll be here in ten minutes—five minutes.' He snarled, a terrified animal.

He had caught sight of their stretcher and snatched at it, thrusting out his face, the face of a terrified animal, open mouth, and round, palpitating eyes. He lifted his hand as though he would have struck at Charlotte, but John pushed him back. He was brutalised, made savage and cruel by terror; he had a lust to hurt.

'You can't have our stretcher,' Charlotte said.

She could see they didn't want it. This was

THE ROMANTIC

the last tram. The serious cases had been sent on first. All these men could walk or hobble along somehow with help. But they were the last in the retreat of the wounded; they were the men who had been nearest to the enemy, and they had known the extremity of fear.

'You can't have it. It's wanted for a badly wounded man.'

'Where is he?'

'We don't know. We're looking for him.'

'Ah, pah! We can't wait till you find him. Do you think we're going to stand here to be taken?—For one man!'

They went on through the plantation, stumbling and growling, dragging the wounded out into the road.

'If,' Charlotte said, 'we only knew where he was.'

John stood there silent; his head was turned towards the far end of the wood, the Lokeren end. The terror of the wood held him. He seemed to be listening; listening, but only half-awake.

Here, where the line stopped, a narrow track led downwards out of the wood. Charlotte started to go along it. 'Come on,' she said. She saw him coming, quickly, but with drawn, sleep-walking feet. The track led into a muddy alley at the back of the village. There was a house there and a woman stood at the door, beckoning. She ran up to them. 'He's here,' she whispered. 'He's here.'

He lay on his side on the flagged floor of the kitchen. His shirt was ripped open, and in his white back, below the shoulder blade, there was a deep red wound, like a pit, with a wide mouth, gaping. He was ugly, a Flamand; he had a puffed face with pushed out lips and a scrub of red beard; but Charlotte loved him.

They carried him out through the wood on to the road. He lay inert, humped up, heavy. They had to go slowly, so slowly that they could see the wounded and the Red Cross men going on far before them, down the street.

The flagged road swayed and swung with the swinging bulge of the stretcher as they staggered. The shafts kept on slipping and slipping; her grasp closed, tighter and tighter; her arms ached in their sockets; but her fingers and the palms of her hands were firm and dry; they could keep their hold.

They had only gone a few yards along the road when suddenly John stopped and sank his

THE ROMANTIC

end of the stretcher, compelling Charlotte to lower hers too.

'What did you do that for?'

'We can't, Charlotte. He's too damned heavy.'

'If I can, you can.'

He didn't move. He stood there, staring with his queer, hypnotised eyes, at the man lying in the middle of the road, at the red pit in the white back, at the wide, ragged lips of the wound, gaping.

'For goodness' sake, pick him up. It isn't the moment for resting.'

'Look here—it isn't good enough. We can't get him there in time.'

'You're—you're *not* going to leave him?'

'We've got to leave him. We can't let the whole lot be taken just for one man.'

'We'll be taken if you stand here talking.'

He went on a step or two, slouching; then stood still, waiting for her, ashamed. He was changed from himself, seized and driven by the fear that had possessed the men in the plantation. She could see it in his retreating eyes.

She cried out—her voice sounded sharp and strange—'John——! You *can't* leave him.'

The wounded man who had lain inert, thinking

that they were only resting, now turned his head at her cry. She saw his eyes shaking, palpitating with terror.

'You've frightened him,' she said. 'I won't have him frightened.'

She didn't really believe that John was going. He went slowly, still ashamed, and stopped again and waited for her.

'Come back,' she said, 'this minute, and pick up that stretcher and get on.'

'I tell you it isn't good enough.'

'Oh, go, then, if you're such a damned coward, and send Mac to me. Or Trixie.'

'They'll have gone.'

He was walking backwards, his face set towards the turn of the road.

'Come on, you little fool. You can't carry him.'

'I can. And I shall, if Mac doesn't come.'

'You'll be taken,' he shouted.

'I don't care. If I'm taken, I'm taken. I shall carry him on my back.'

While John still went backwards she thought: It's all right. If he sees I'm not coming he won't go. He'll come back to the stretcher.

But John had turned and was running.

Even then she didn't realise that he was running

THE ROMANTIC

away, that she was left there with the wounded man. Things didn't happen like that. People ran away all of a sudden, in panics, because they couldn't help it; they didn't begin by going slowly and stopping to argue and turning round and walking backwards; they were gone before they knew where they were. She believed that he was going for the ambulance. One moment she believed it and the next she knew better. As she waited in the road (conscious of the turn, the turn with its curving screen of tall trees) her knowledge, her dreadful knowledge came to her, dark and evil, creeping up and up. John wasn't coming back. He would no more come back than he had come back the other day. Sutton had come. The other day had been like to-day. John was like that.

Her mind stood still in amazement, seeing, seeing clearly, what John was like. For a moment she forgot about the Germans.

She thought: I don't believe Mac's gone. He wouldn't go until he'd got them all in. Mac would come.

Then she thought about the Germans again. All this was making it much more dangerous for Mac and everybody, with the Germans coming round the corner any minute; she had no business to stand there thinking; she must pick that man up on her back and go on.

She stooped down and turned him over on his chest. Then, with great difficulty, she got him up on to his feet; she took him by the wrists and, stooping again, swung him on to her shoulder. These acts, requiring attention and drawing on all her energy, dulled the pain of her knowledge. When she stood up with him she saw John and McClane coming to her. She lowered her man gently back on to the stretcher. The Flamand, thinking that she had given it up and that he was now abandoned to the Germans, groaned.

'It's all right,' she said. 'He's coming.'

She saw McClane holding John by the arm, and in her pain there was a sharper pang. She had the illusion of his being dragged back unwillingly.

McClane smiled as he came to her. He glanced at the Flamand lying heaped on his stretcher.

'He's been too much for you, has he?'

'Too much——? Yes.'

Instantly she saw that John had lied, and instantly she backed his lie. She hated McClane thinking she had failed; but anything was better than his knowing the truth.

THE ROMANTIC

John and McClane picked up the stretcher and went on quickly. Charlotte walked beside the Flamand with her hand on his shoulder to comfort him. Again her pity was like love.

From the top of the village she could see the opening of the lane. Down there was the house with the tall green door where the dead man was. John had *said* he was dead.

Supposing he wasn't? Or supposing he was still warm and limp like the boy at Melle? She must know; it was a thing she must know for certain, or she would never have any peace. And when the Flamand was laid out on McClane's table, while McClane dressed his wound, she slipped down the lane and opened the green door.

The man lay on a row of packing cases with his feet parted. She put one hand over his heart and the other on his forehead under the lock of blood-stained hair. He was dead: stiff dead and cold. His tunic and shirt had been unbuttoned to ease his last breathing. She had a queer baffled feeling of surprise and incompleteness, as if some awful sense in her would have been satisfied if she had seen that he had been living when John had said that he was dead. To-day would then have been linked on firmly to the other day.

John stood at the top of the lane. He scowled at her as she came.

'What do you think you're doing?' he said.

'I went to that house—to see if the man was dead.'

'You'd no business to. I told you he was dead.'

'I wanted to make sure.'

That evening she had just gone to her room when somebody knocked at her door. McClane stood outside, straddling, his way when he had something important on hand. He asked if he might come in and speak to her for a minute.

She sat down on the edge of her bed and he sat on Gwinnie's, elbows crooked out, hands planted on wide-parted knees; he leaned forward, looking at her, his face innocent and yet astute; his thick, expressionless eyes clear now and penetrating. He seemed to be fairly humming with activity left over from the excitement of the day. He was always either dreamy and withdrawn, or bursting, bursting with energy, and at odd moments he would drop off suddenly to sleep

THE ROMANTIC

with his chin doubled on his breast, recovering from his energy. Perhaps he had just waked up now to this freshness.

'Look here,' he said. 'You didn't break down. That man wasn't too heavy for you.'

'He was. He was an awful weight. I couldn't have carried him a yard.'

'That won't do, Charlotte. I *saw* you take him on your back.'

She could feel the blood rising up in her face before him. He was hurting her with shame.

He persisted, merciless. 'It was Conway who broke down.'

She had tears now.

'Nobody knows,' he said gently, 'but you and me. . . . I want to talk to you about him. He must be got away from the front. He must be got out of Belgium.'

'You always wanted to get him away.'

'Only because I saw he would break down.'

'How could you tell?'

'I'm a psychotherapist. It's my business to tell.'

But she was still on the defensive.

'You never liked him.'

'I neither like nor dislike him. To me

JOHN RODEN. CONWAY

Conway is simply a sick man. If I could cure him——'

'Can't you?'

'Not as you think. I can't turn his cowardice into courage. I might turn it into something else, but not that. That's why I say he ought to go home. You must tell him.'

'I can't. Couldn't Billy tell him?'

'Well, hardly. He's his commandant.'

'Can't *you*?'

'Not I. You know what he thinks about me.'

'What?'

'That I've got a grudge against him. That I'm jealous of him. You thought it yourself.'

'Did I?'

'You did. Look here, I say—I wanted to take you three into my corps. And you'd have been sent home after that Berlaere affair if I hadn't spoken for you. So much for my jealousy.'

'I only thought you were jealous of John.'

'Why, it was I who got him sent out that first day.'

'*Was* it?'

'Yes. I wanted to give him his chance. And,' he added meditatively, 'I wanted to know whether I was right. I wanted to see what he would do.'

'I don't think it now,' she said, reverting.

'*That's* all right.'

He laughed his brief, mirthless laugh, the assent of his egoism. But his satisfaction had nothing personal in it. He was pleased because justice, abstract justice, had been done. But she suspected his sincerity. He did things for you, not because he liked you, but for some other reason; and he would be so carried away by doing them that he would behave as though he liked you when he didn't, when all the time you couldn't for one minute rouse him from his immense indifference. She knew he liked her for sticking to her post and for taking the wounded man on her back, because that was the sort of thing he would have done himself. And he had only helped John because he wanted to see what he would do. Therefore she suspected his sincerity.

But, no; he wasn't jealous.

'And now,' he went on, 'you must get him to go home at once, or he'll have a bad breakdown. You've got to tell him, Charlotte.'

She stood up, ready. 'Where is he?'

JOHN RODEN CONWAY

'By himself. In his room.'

She went to him there.

He was sitting at his little table. He had been trying to write a letter, but he had pushed it from him and left it. You could see he was absorbed in some bitter meditation. She seated herself at the head of his bed, on his pillow, where she could look down at him.

'John,' she said, 'you can't go on like this——'

'Like what?'

He held his head high; but the excited, happy light had gone out of his eyes; they stared, not as though they saw anything, but withdrawn, as though he were contemplating the fearful memory of his fear.

And she was sorry for him, so sorry that she couldn't bear it. She bit her lip lest she should sob out with pain.

'Oh——' she said, and her pain stopped her.

'I don't know what you're talking about—"going on like this." I'm—going—on.'

'What's the good? You've had enough. If I were you I should go home. You know you can't stand it.'

'What? Go and leave my cars to Sutton?'

THE ROMANTIC

'McClane could take them.'

'I don't know how long McClane signed on for. *I* signed on for the duration of the war.'

'There wasn't any signing on.'

'Well, if you like, I swore I wouldn't go back till it was over.'

'Yes, and supposing it happens again.'

'What *should* happen again?'

'What happened this afternoon. . . . And it wasn't the first time.'

'Do you *know* what happened?'

'I *saw* what happened. You simply went to pieces.'

'My dear Charlotte, *you* went to pieces, if you like.'

'I know that's what you told Mac. And *he* knows how true it is.'

'Does he? Well—he shan't have my ambulances. You don't suppose I'm going to let McClane fire me out of Belgium? . . . I suppose he put you up to this. . . .'

He stood up as a sign to her to leave him. 'I don't see that there's anything more to be said.'

'There's one thing.' (She slid to her feet.) '*You* swore you'd stick it till the war's over. *I* swore, if I had to choose between you and the wounded, it shouldn't be you.'

'You haven't got to choose. You've only got to obey orders. . . .'

His face stiffened. He looked like some hard commander imposing an unanswerable will.

'. . . The next time,' he said, ' you'll be good enough to remember that I settle what risks are to be taken, not you.'

Her soul stiffened, too, and was hard. She stood up against him with her shoulder to the door.

'It sounds all right,' she said. 'But *next time* I'll carry him on my back all the way.'

She went to bed with her knowledge. He funked and lied. The two things she couldn't stand. His funk and his lying were a real part of him. And it was as if she had always known it, as if all the movements of her mind had been an effort to escape her knowledge.

She opened her eyes. Something hurt them. Gwinnie, coming late to bed, had turned on the electric light. And as she rolled over, turning her back to the light and to Gwinnie, her mind shifted. It saw suddenly the flame leaping in

THE ROMANTIC

John's face. His delight in danger, that happiness he felt when he went out to meet it, happiness springing up bright and new every day; that was a real part of him. She couldn't doubt it. She knew. And she was left with her queer, baffled sense of surprise and incompleteness. She couldn't see the nature of the bond between these two realities.

That was his secret, his mystery.

XII

She woke very early in the morning with one clear image in her mind: what John had done yesterday.

Her mind seemed to have watched all night behind her sleep to attack her with it in the first moment of waking. She had got to come to a clear decision about that. If Billy Sutton had done it, or one of McClane's chauffeurs, her decision would have been very clear. She would have said he was a filthy coward and dismissed him from her mind. But John couldn't be dismissed. His funk wasn't like other people's funk. Coupled with his ecstatic love of danger it had an unreal, fantastic quality. Somehow she couldn't regard his love of danger as an unreal, fantastic thing. It had come too near her; it had moved her too profoundly and too long; she had shared it as she might have shared his passion.

So that, even in the sharp, waking day she felt his fear as a secret, mysterious thing. She

THE ROMANTIC

couldn't account for it. She didn't, considering the circumstances, she didn't judge the imminence of the Germans to be a sufficient explanation. It was as incomprehensible to-day as it had been yesterday.

But there was fear and fear. There was the cruel, animal fear of the Belgians in the plantation, fear that was dark to itself and had no sadness in it; and there was John's fear that knew itself and was sad. The unbearable, inconsolable sadness of John's fear! After all, you could think of him as a gentle thing, caught unaware in a trap and tortured. And who was she to judge him? She in her 'armour' and he in his coat of nerves. His knowledge and his memory of his fear would be like a raw open wound in his mind; and her knowledge of it would be a perpetual irritant, rubbing against it and keeping up the sore. Last night she hadn't done anything to heal him; she had only hurt. . . . And if she gave John up his wound would never heal. She owed a sort of duty to the wound.

Of course, like John, she would go on remembering what had happened yesterday. She would never get over it any more than he would. Yet, after all, yesterday was only one day out of his life. There might never be another like it. And to set against yesterday there was their first day at Berlaere and the day afterwards at Melle; there was yesterday morning and there was that other day at Melle. She had no business to suppose that he had done then what he did yesterday. They had settled that once for all at the time, when he said Billy Sutton had told him she was going back with him. It all hung on that. If that was right, the rest was right. . . .

Supposing Billy hadn't told him anything of the sort, though? She would never know that. She couldn't say to Billy, '*Did* you tell John I was going back with you? Because; if you didn't———' She would have to leave that as it was, not quite certain. . . . And she couldn't be quite certain whether the boy had been dead or alive. And. . . . No. She couldn't get over it, John's cowardice. It had destroyed the unique, beautiful happiness she had had with him.

For it was no use saying that courage, physical courage, didn't count. She could remember a long conversation she had had with George Corfield, the man who wanted to marry her, about that. He had said courage was the least thing you could have. That only meant that, whatever else you hadn't, you must have that. It was a sort of trust. You were trusted not to betray defenceless things. A coward was a person who betrayed defenceless things. George had said that the world's adoration of courage was the world's cowardice, its fear of betrayal. That was a question for cowards to settle among themselves. The obligation not to betray defenceless things remained. It was so simple and obvious that people took it for granted; they didn't talk about it. They didn't talk about it because it was so deep and sacred, like honour and like love; so that, when John had talked about it she had always felt that he was her lover, saying the things that other men might not say, things he couldn't have said to any other woman.

It was inconceivable that he—— It couldn't have happened. As he had said of the defeat of Belgium, it was so bad that it couldn't happen. Odd, that the other day she had accepted at once a thing she didn't know for certain, while now she fought fiercely against a thing she knew; and always the memory of it, returning, beat her down.

She had to make up her mind on what terms she would live with it and whether she could live with it at all. Supposing it happened again? Supposing you had always to go in fear of its happening? . . . It mightn't happen. Funk might be a thing that attacked you like an illness, or like drink, in fits, with long, calm intervals between. She wondered what it would feel like to be subject to attacks. Perhaps you would recover; you would be on the look-out, and when you felt another fit coming on you could stave it off or fight it down. And the first time wouldn't count because you had had no warning. It wouldn't be fair to give him up because of the first time.

He would have given *her* up, he would have left her to the Germans—yes; but if she broke with him now she would never get beyond that thought, she would never get beyond yesterday; she would always see it, the flagged road swinging with the swinging bulge of the stretcher, the sudden stopping, the Flamand with his wound, the shafts of the stretcher, suddenly naked, sticking out; and then all the fantastic, incredible movements of John's flight. Her mind would separate from him on that, closing everything down, making his act eternal.

And, after all, the Germans hadn't come round the corner. Perhaps he wouldn't have left her if they had really come. How did she know what he wouldn't have done?

No. That was thin. Thin. She couldn't take herself in quite in that way. It was the way she had tried with Gibson Herbert. When he did anything she loathed she used to pretend he hadn't done it. But with John, if she didn't give him up, her eyes must always be open. Perhaps they would get beyond yesterday. Perhaps she would see other things, go on with him to something new, forgetting. Her unique, beautiful happiness was smashed. Still, there might be some other happiness, beautiful, though not with the same beauty.

If John got the better of his fear—She thought of all the men she had ever heard of who had done that, coming out in the end heroic, triumphant.

Three things, three little things that happened that morning, that showed the way his mind was working. Things that she couldn't get over, that she would never forget.

John standing on the hospital steps, watching Trixie Rankin and Alice Bartrum as they started with the ambulance; the fierce fling of his body, turning away.

JOHN RODEN CONWAY

His voice saying, ' I loathe those women. There's Alice Bartrum—I saw her making eyes at Sutton over a spouting artery. As for Mrs Rankin they ought to intern her. She oughtn't to be allowed within ten miles of any army. That's one thing I like about McClane. He can't stand that sort of thing any more than I can.'

' How about Gwinnie and me ? '

' Gwinnie hangs her beastly legs about all over the place. So do you.'

John, standing at the foot of the stairs, looking at the Antwerp men. Their heads and faces were covered with a white mask of cotton wool like a diver's helmet, three small holes in each white mask for mouth and eyes. They were the men whose faces had been burned by fire at Antwerp.

' Come away,' she said. But he still stood, fascinated, hypnotised by the white masks.

' If I were to stick there, doing nothing, looking at the wounded, I should go off my head.'

' My God! So should I. Those everlasting wounds. They make you dream about them. Disgusting dreams. I never really see the wound, but I'm just going to see it. I know it's going to be more horrible than any wound I've

THE ROMANTIC

ever seen. And then I wake. . . . That's why I don't look at them more than I can help.'

'You're looking at them now,' she said.

'Oh, them. That's nothing. Cotton wool.'

And she, putting her hand on his arm to draw him up the stairs, away. John shaking her hands off and his queer voice rising. 'I wish you wouldn't do that, Charlotte. You know I hate it.'

He had never said anything to her like that before. It hadn't struck her before that, changed to himself, he would change to her. He hadn't got over last night. She had hurt him; her knowledge of his cowardice hurt him; and this was how he showed his pain.

She thought: Here's Antwerp falling and Belgium beaten. And all those wounded. And the dead. . . . And here am I, bothering about these little things, as if they mattered. Three little things.

The fire from the battlefield had raked the village street as they came in; but it had ceased now. The *curé* had been through it all, going up and down, helping with the stretchers. John was down there in the wine-shop, where the soldiers were, looking for more wounded.

They had found five in the stable yard, waiting to be taken away; they had moved four of them into the ambulance. The fifth, shot through the back of his head, still lay on the ground on a stretcher that dripped blood. Charlotte stood beside him.

The *curé* came to her there. He was slender and lean in his black cassock. He had a Red Cross brassard on his sleeve, and in one hand he carried his missal and in the other the Host and the holy oils in a little bag of purple silk. He looked down at the stretcher and he looked at Charlotte, smiling faintly.

'Where is monsieur?' he said.

'In the wine-shop, looking for wounded.'

She thought: He isn't looking for them. He's skulking there, out of the firing. He'll always be like that.

It had begun again. The bullets whistled in the air and rapped on the stone causeway, and ceased. The *curé* glanced down the street towards the place they had come from and smiled again.

She liked his lean, dark face and the long lines that came in it when it smiled. It despised the firing, it despised death, it despised everything that could be done to him there. And it was utterly compassionate.

THE ROMANTIC

'Then,' he said, 'it is for you and me to carry him, mademoiselle.' He stooped to the stretcher.

Between them they lifted him very slowly and gently into the ambulance.

'There, monsieur, at the bottom.'

At the bottom because of the steady drip, drip that no bandaging could stanch. He lay straight and stiff, utterly unconcerned, and his feet in their enormous boots, slightly parted, stuck out beyond the stretcher. The four others sat in a row down one side of the car and stared at him.

The *curé* climbed in after him, carrying the Host. He knelt there, where the blood from the smashed head oozed through the bandages and through the canvas of the stretchers to the floor and to the skirts of his cassock.

The Last Sacrament. Charlotte waited till it was over, standing stolidly by the tail of the car. She could have cried then because of the sheer beauty of the *curé's* act, even while she wondered whether perhaps the wafer on his tongue might not choke the dying man.

The *curé* hovered on the edge of the car, stooping with a certain awkwardness; she took from him his missal and his purple bag as he gathered his cassock about him and came down.

'Can I do anything, monsieur?'

'No, mademoiselle. It *is* done.'

His eyes smiled at her; but his lips were quivering as he took again his missal and his purple bag. She watched him going on slowly down the street till he turned into the wine-shop. She wondered: Had he seen? Did he know why John was there? In another minute John came out, hurrying to the car.

He glanced down at the bloodstains by the back step; then he looked in; and when he saw the man lying on the stretcher he turned on her in fury.

'What are you thinking of? I told you you weren't to take him.'

'I had to. I couldn't leave him there. I thought——'

'You've no business to think.'

'Well, the *curé*——'

'The *curé* doesn't know anything about it.'

'I don't care. If he's in a clean bed—if they take his boots off——'

'I told you they can't spare clean beds for corpses. He'll be dead before you can get him there.'

'Not if we're quick.'

'Nonsense. We must get him out of that.'

THE ROMANTIC

He seized the handle of the stretcher and began pulling; she hung on to his arm and stopped that.

'No. No,' she said. 'You shan't touch him.'

He flung her arm off and turned. 'You fool,' he said. 'You fool.'

She looked at him steadily, a long look that remembered, that made him remember.

'There isn't time,' she said. 'They'll begin *firing* in another minute.'

'Damn you.' But he had turned, slinking round the corner of the hood to the engine. While he cranked it up she thought of the kit that one of the men had left there in the yard. She made a dash and fetched it, and as she threw it on the floor the car started. She snatched at the rope and swung herself up on to the step. The dying man lay behind her, straight and stiff; his feet in their heavy boots stuck out close under her hand.

The four men nodded and grinned at her. They protected her. They understood.

If only she could get him into a clean bed. If only she had had time to take his boots off. It would be all right if only she could bring him in alive.

JOHN RODEN CONWAY

He was still alive when they got into Ghent.

She had forgotten John and it was not until they came to take out the stretcher that she was again aware of him. They had drawn up before the steps of the hospital; he had got down and was leaning sideways, staring under the stretcher.

'What is it?'

'You can see what it is. Blood.'

From the hole in the man's head, through the soaked bandages, it still dripped, dripped with a light sound; it had made a glairy pool on the floor of the ambulance.

'Don't look at it,' she said. 'It'll make you sick. You know you can't stand it.'

'Oh. I can't *stand* it, can't I?'

He straightened himself. He threw back his head; his upper lip lifted, stretched tight and thin above the clean white teeth. His eyes looked down at her, narrowed, bright slits under dropped lids.

'John—I want to get him in before he dies.'

'All right. Get in under there. Take his head.'

'Hadn't I better take his feet?'

'You'd better take what you're told to.'

She stiffened to the weight, heaved up her

THE ROMANTIC

shoulder. Two men came running down the steps to help her as John pulled.

'They'll be glad,' he said, 'to see him.'

She was in the yard of the hospital, swabbing out the car, when John came to her.

The back and side of the hospital, the long barracks of the annex and the wall at the bottom enclosed a waste place of ochreish clay. A long wooden shed, straw-white and new, was built out under the red brick of the annex. She thought it was a garage. John came out of the door of the shed. He beckoned to her as he came.

'Come here,' he said. 'I want to show you something.'

They went close together, John gripping her arm, in the old way, to steer her. As they came to the long wall of the shed his eyes slewed round and looked at her out of their corners. She had seen that sidelong, attentive look once before, when she was a little girl, in the eyes of a school-boy who had taken her away and told her something horrid. The door of the shed stood ajar. John half led, half pushed her in.

'Look there——' he said.

The dead men were laid out in a row, on their

backs; grayish white, sallow-white faces upturned; bodies straight and stiff on a thin litter of straw. Pale gray light hovered, filtered through dust.

It came from some clearer place of glass beyond that might have been a carpenter's shop, partitioned off. She couldn't see what was going on there. She didn't see anything but the dead bodies, the dead faces, and John's living face.

He leaned against the wall; his head was thrown back, his eyes moved glistening under the calm lids; the corners of his mouth and the wings of his nostrils were lifted as he laughed: a soft thin laugh, breathed out between the edges of his teeth. He pointed.

'There's your man. Shows how much they wanted him, doesn't it?'

He lay there, the last comer, in his uniform and bloody bandages, his stiff, peaked mouth open, his legs stretched apart as they had sprung in his last agony.

'Oh, John———'

She cried out in her fright and put her hand over her eyes. She had always been afraid of the dead bodies. She didn't want to know where they put them, and nobody had told her.

John gripped her wrists so that he hurt her

THE ROMANTIC

and dragged down her hands. He looked into her eyes, still laughing.

'I thought you weren't afraid of anything,' he said.

'I'm not afraid when we're out there. I'm only afraid of *seeing* them. You know I am.'

She turned, but he had put himself between her and the door. She wrenched at the latch, sobbing.

'How could you be so *cruel*? What did you do it for? What did you *do* it for?'

'I wanted you to see what they've done with him. There's his clean bed. They haven't even taken his boots off.'

'You brute! You *utter* brute!'

A steely sound like a dropped hammer came from behind the glass partition; then the sliding of a latch. John opened the door a little way and she slipped out past him.

'*Next time*,' he said, 'perhaps you'll do as you're told.'

She wanted to get away by herself. Not into her own room, where Gwinnie, who had been unloading ambulance trains half the night, now rested. The McClane Corps was crowding into the messroom for tea. She passed through

JOHN RODEN CONWAY

without looking at any of them and out on to the balcony, closing the French window behind her. She could hide there beyond the window where the wall was blank.

She leaned back, flattening herself against the wall. . . .

Something would have to be done. They couldn't go on like this. . . . Her mind went to and fro, quickly, with short, jerky movements, distressed; it had to do so much thinking in so short a time.

She would always have to reckon with John's fear. And John's fear was not what she had thought it, a sad, helpless, fatal thing, sad because it knew itself doom-like and helpless. It was cruel, with a sort of mental violence in it, worse than the cruel animal fear of the men in the plantation. She could see that his cowardice had something to do with his cruelty and that his cruelty was somehow linked up with his cowardice; but she couldn't for the life of her imagine the secret of the bond. She only felt that it would be something secret and horrible; something that she would rather not know about.

And she knew that since yesterday he had left off caring for her. His love had died a sudden, cruel, and violent death. His cowardice had

THE ROMANTIC

done that too. . . . And he had left off caring for the wounded. It was almost as if he hated them, because they lay so still, keeping him back, keeping him out under the fire.

Queer, but all those other cowardly things that he had done had seemed to her unreal even when she had seen him doing them; and afterwards when she thought about them they were unreal, as if they hadn't happened, as if she had just imagined them. Incredible, and yet the sort of thing you *could* imagine if you tried. But that last devilish thing he did, it had a hard, absolute reality. Just because it was inconceivable, because you couldn't have imagined it, you couldn't doubt that it had happened.

It was happening now. As long as she lived it would go on happening in her mind. She would never get away from it.

There were things that men did, bestial things, cruel things, things they did to women. But not things like this. They didn't think of them, because this thing wasn't thinkable.

Why had John done it? Why? She supposed he wanted to hurt her and frighten her because he had been hurt, because he had been frightened. And because he knew she loved her wounded men. Perhaps he wanted to make her hate him and have done with it.

Well, she did hate him. Oh, yes, she hated him.

She heard the window open and shut and a woman's footsteps swishing on the stone floor. Trixie Rankin came to her, with her quick look that fell on you like a bird swooping. She stood facing her, upright and stiff in her sharp beauty; her lips were pressed together as though they had just closed on some biting utterance; but her eyes were soft and intent.

'What's he done this time?' she said.

'He hasn't done anything.'

'Oh, yes, he has. He's done something perfectly beastly.'

It was no use lying to Trixie. She knew what he was like, even if she didn't know about yesterday, even if she didn't know what he had done now. Nobody could know that. She looked straight at Trixie, with broad, open eyes that defied her to know.

'What makes you think so?'

'Your face.'

'Damn my face. It's got nothing to do with you, Trixie.'

'Yes, it has. If it gives the show away I can't help seeing, can I?'

THE ROMANTIC

'You can help talking.'

'Yes, I can help talking.'

The arrogance had gone out of her face. It could change in a minute from the face of a bird of prey to the face of a watching angel. It looked at her as it looked at wounded men: tender and protective. But Trixie couldn't see that you didn't want any tenderness and protection just then, or any recognition of your wound.

'You rum little blighter,' she said. 'Come along. Nobody's going to talk.'

There was a stir as Charlotte went in; people shifting their places to make room for her; McClane calling out to her to come and sit by him; Alice Bartrum making sweet eyes; the men getting up and cutting bread and butter and reaching for her cup to give it her. She could see they were all determined to be nice, to show her what they thought of her; they had sent Trixie to bring her in. There was something a little deliberate about it and exaggerated. They were getting it up—a demonstration in her favour, a demonstration against John Conway.

She talked; but her thoughts ran by themselves on a line separate from her speech.

'We got in six wounded.' . . . 'That *curé* was there again. He was splendid.' . . . They didn't know anything. They condemned him on the evidence of her face, the face she had brought back to them, coming straight from John. Her face had the mark of what he had done to her. . . . ' Much firing ? Not so very much.' . . . She remembered what he had said to her about her face. ' Something's happened to it. Some cruelty. Some damnable cruelty. . . .'

' We'll have to go out there again.'

They were all listening, and Alice Bartrum had made fresh tea for her; McClane was setting down her cup. She was thirsty; she longed for the fresh, fragrant tea; she was soothed by the kind, listening faces. Suddenly they drew away; they weren't listening any more. John had come into the room.

It flashed on her that all these people thought that John was her lover, her lover in the way they understood love. They were looking at him as if they hated him. But John's face was quiet and composed and somehow triumphant; it held itself up against all the hostile faces; it fronted McClane and his men as their equal; it was the face of a man who has satisfied a lust. His whole body had a look of assurance and accomplishment, as if his cruelty had given him power.

THE ROMANTIC

And with it all he kept his dreadful beauty. It hurt her to look at him.

She rose, leaving her tea untasted, and went out of the room. She couldn't sit there with him. She had given him up. Her horror of him was pure, absolute. It would never return on itself to know pity or remorse.

XIII

And the next day, as if nothing had happened, he was excited and eager to set out. He could sleep off his funk in the night, like drink, and get up in the morning as if it had never been. He was more immune from memory than any drunkard. He woke to his romance as a child wakes to the renewed wonder of the world. It was so real to him that, however hardly you judged him, you couldn't think of him as a humbug or a hypocrite. . . . No. He was not that. He was not that. His mind truly lived in a glorious state for which none of his disgraceful deeds were ever done. It created a sort of innocence for him. She could forgive him (even after yesterday), she could almost believe in him again when she saw him coming down the hall to the ambulance with his head raised and his eyes shining, gallant and keen.

They were to go to Berlaere. Trixie Rankin had gone on before them with Gurney, McClane's

THE ROMANTIC

best chauffeur. McClane and Sutton were at Melle.

They had not been to Berlaere since that day, the first time they had gone out together. That time at least had been perfect; it remained secure; nothing could ever spoil it; she could remember the delight of it, their strange communion of ecstasy, without doubt, without misgiving. She could never forget. It might have been better if she could, instead of knowing that it would exist in her for ever, to torment her by its unlikeness to the days, the awful, incredible days that had come afterwards. There was no way of thinking that John had been more real that day than he had been yesterday. She was simply left with the inscrutable mystery of him on her hands. But she could see clearly that he was more real to himself. Yesterday and the day before had ceased to exist for him. He was back in his old self.

There was only one sign of memory that he gave. He was no longer her lover; he no longer recognised her even as his comrade. He was her commandant. It was his place to command, and hers to be commanded. He looked at her, when he looked at her at all, with a stern coldness. She was a woman who had committed some grave fault, whom he no longer trusted. So masterly was his playing of this part, so great, in a way, was still his power over her, that there were moments when she almost believed in the illusion he created. She had committed some grave fault. She was not worthy of his trust. Somewhere, at some time forgotten, in some obscure and secret way, she had betrayed him.

She had so mixed her hidden self with his in love that even now, with all her knowledge of him, she couldn't help feeling the thing as he felt it and seeing as he saw. Her mind kept on passing in and out of the illusion with little shocks of astonishment.

And yet all the time she was acutely aware of the difference. When she went out with him she felt that she was going with something dangerous and uncertain. She knew what fear was now. She was afraid all the time of what he would do next, of what he would not do. Her wounded were not safe with him. Nothing was safe.

She wished that she could have gone out with Billy; with Billy there wouldn't be any excitement, but neither would there be this abominable fear. On the other hand, you couldn't let anybody else take the risk of John; and you couldn't,

THE ROMANTIC

you simply couldn't, let him go alone. Conceive him going alone—the things that might happen; she could at least see that some things didn't.

It was odd, but John had never shown the smallest desire to go without her. If he hadn't liked it he could easily have taken Sutton or Gwinnie or one of the McClane men. It was as if, in spite of his hostility, he still felt, as he had said, that where she was everything would be right.

And it looked as if this time nothing would go wrong. When they came into the village the firing had stopped; it was concentrating farther east, towards Zele. Trixie's ambulance was packed, and Trixie was excited and triumphant.

Her gestures waved them back as useless, much too late; without them she had got in all the wounded. But in the end they took over two of them, slight cases that Trixie resigned without a pang. She had had to turn them out to make room for poor Gurney, the chauffeur, who had hurt himself, ruptured something, slipping on a muddy bank with his stretcher.

Mr Conway, she said, could drive her back to Ghent and Charlotte could follow with the

JOHN RODEN CONWAY

two men. She had settled it all, in her bright, domineering way, in a second, and now swung herself up on the back step of her car.

They had got round the turn of the village and Charlotte was starting to follow them when she heard them draw up. In another minute John appeared, walking back slowly down the street with a young Belgian lieutenant. They were talking earnestly together. So soon as Charlotte saw the lieutenant she had a sense of something happening, something fatal, that would change Trixie's safe, easy programme. John, as he came on, looked perturbed and thoughtful. They stopped. The lieutenant was saying something final. John nodded assent and saluted. The lieutenant sketched a salute and hurried away in the opposite direction.

John waited till he was well out of sight before he came to her. (She noticed that.) He had the look at first of being up to something, as if the devil of yesterday was with him still.

It passed. His voice had no devil in it. 'I say, I've got a job for you, Charlotte. Something you'll like.'

There was no devil in his voice, but he stared away from her as he spoke.

THE ROMANTIC

'I don't want you to go to Ghent. I want you to go on to Zele.'

'Zele? Do I know the way?'

'It's quite easy. You turn round and go the way we went that first day—you remember? It's the shortest cut from here.'

'Pretty bad going, though. Hadn't we better go on and strike the main road?'

'Yes, if you want to go miles round and get held up by the transport.'

'All right—if we can get through.'

'You'll get through all right.' His voice had the tone of finality.

'I'm to go by myself, then?'

'Well—if I've got to drive Mrs Rankin——'

She thought: It's going to be dangerous.

'By the way, I haven't told her I'm sending you. You don't want her butting in and going with you.'

'No. I certainly don't want Trixie. . . . And look here, I don't particularly want those men. Much better leave them here where they're safe and send in again for them.'

'I don't know that I *can* send in again. We're supposed to have finished this job. The cars may be wanted for anything. *They*'ll be all right.'

'I don't *like* taking them.'

'You're making difficulties,' he said. He was irritable and hurried; he had kept on turning and looking up the street as though he thought the lieutenant might appear again at any minute.

'When *will* you learn that you've simply got to obey orders?'

'All right.'

She hadn't a chance with him. Whatever she said and did he could always bring it round to that, her orders. She thought she knew what *his* orders had been.

He cranked up the engine. She could see him stooping and rising to it, a rhythmic elastic movement; he was cranking energetically, with a sort of furious, flushed enjoyment of his power.

She backed and turned, and he ran forward with her as she started. He shouted: 'Don't think about the main road. Get through. . . . And hurry *up*. You haven't got too much time.'

She knew. It was going to be dangerous and he funked it. He hadn't got to drive Trixie into Ghent. When the worst came to the worst Trixie could drive herself. She thought: He

THE ROMANTIC

didn't tell her because he daren't. He knew she wouldn't let him send me by myself. She'd *make* him go. She'd stand over him and bully him till he had to.

Still, she could do it. She could get through. Going by herself was better than going with a man who funked it. Only she would have liked it better without the two wounded men. She thought of them, jostled, falling against each other, falling forward and recovering, shaken by the jolting of the car, and perhaps brought back into danger. She suspected that not having too much time might be the essence of the risk.

Everything was quiet as they ran along the open road from the village to the hamlet that sat low and humble on the edge of the fields. A few houses and the long wall of the barn still stood; but by this time the house she had brought the guns from had the whole of its roof knocked in, and the stripped gable at the end of the row no longer pricked up its point against the sky; the front of the hollow shell had fallen forward and flung itself across the road.

For a moment she thought the way was blocked. She thought: If I can't get round I must get over. She backed, charged, and the car, rocking a little, struggled through. And there, where the road swerved slightly, the high wall of a barn, undermined, bulged forward, toppling. It answered the vibration of the car with a visible tremor. So soon as she passed it fell with a great crash and rumbling and sprawled in a smoky heap that blocked her way behind her.

After that they went through quiet country for a time; but farther east, near the town, the shelling began. The road here was opened up into great holes with ragged, hollow edges; she had to skirt them carefully, and sometimes there would not be enough clear ground to move in, and one wheel of the car would go unsupported, hanging over space.

Yet she had got through.

As she came into Zele she met the last straggling line of the refugees. They cried out to her not to go on. She thought: I must get those men before the retreat begins.

Returning with her heavy load of wounded, on the pitch black road, half-way to Ghent she was halted. She had come up with the tail end of the retreat.

Trixie Rankin stood on the hospital steps looking out. The car turned in and swung up

THE ROMANTIC

the rubber incline, but instead of stopping before the porch, it ran on towards the downward slope. Charlotte jammed on the brakes with a hard jerk and backed to the level.

She couldn't think how she had let the car do that. She couldn't think why she was slipping from the edge of it into Trixie's arms. And stumbling in that ignominious way on the steps with Trixie holding her up on one side. . . . It didn't last. After she had drunk the hot black coffee that Alice Bartrum gave her she was all right.

The men had gone out of the messroom, leaving them alone.

'I'm all right, Trixie, only a bit tired.'

'Tired? I should think you *were* tired. That Conway man's a perfect devil. Fancy scooting back himself on a safe trip and sending you out to Zele. *Zele!*'

'McClane doesn't care much where he sends *you*.'

'Oh, Mac—as if he could stop us. But he'd draw the line at Zele, with the Germans coming into it.'

'Rot. They weren't coming in for hours and hours.'

'Well, anyhow he thought they were.'

JOHN RODEN CONWAY

'He didn't think anything about it. I wanted to go and I went. He—he couldn't stop me.'

'It's no good lying to me, Charlotte. I know too much. I know he had orders to go to Zele himself and the damned coward funked it. I've a good mind to report him to Headquarters.'

'No. You won't do that. You wouldn't be such a putrid beast.'

'If I don't, Charlotte, it's because I like you. You're the pluckiest little blighter in the world. But I'll tell you what I *shall* do. Next time your Mr Conway's ordered on a job he doesn't fancy I'll go with him and hold his nose down to it by the scruff of his neck. If he was *my* man I'd bloody well tell him what I thought of him.'

'It doesn't matter what you think of him. You were pretty well gone on him yourself once.'

'When? When?'

'When you wanted to turn Mac out and make him commandant.'

'Oh, *then*—I was a jolly fool to be taken in by him. So were you.'

She stopped on her way to the door. 'I admit he *looks* everything he isn't. But that only shows what a beastly humbug the man is.'

THE ROMANTIC

'No. He isn't a humbug. He really likes going out, even if he can't stand it when he gets there.'

'I've no use for that sort of courage.'

'It isn't courage. But it isn't humbug.'

'I've no use for your fine distinctions either.'

She heard Alice Bartrum's voice calling to Trixie as she went out, 'It's jolly decent of her not to go back on him.'

The voice went on. 'You needn't mind what Trixie says about cold feet. She's said it about everybody. About Sutton and Mac, and all our men, and me.'

She thought: What's the good of lying when they all know? Still, there were things they wouldn't know if she kept on lying, things they would never guess.

'Trixie doesn't know anything about him,' she said. 'No more do you. You don't know what he *was*.'

'Whatever he *is*, whatever he's done, Charlotte, you mustn't let it hurt you. It hasn't anything to do with you. We all know what *you* are.'

'Me? I'm not bothering about myself. I tell you it's not what *you* think about him, it's what *I* think.'

'Yes,' said Alice Bartrum. Then Gwinnie

JOHN RODEN CONWAY

Denning and John Conway came in and she left them.

John carried himself very straight, and again Charlotte saw about him that odd look of accomplishment and satisfaction.

'So you got through?' he said.

'Yes. I got through.' They kept their eyes from each other as they spoke.

Gwinnie struck in, 'Are you all right?'

'Yes, rather. . . The little Belgian Army doctor was there. He was adorable, sticking on, working away with his wounded, in a sort of heavenly peace, with the Germans just outside.'

'How many did you get?'

'Eleven—thirteen.'

'Oh, good. . . . I've the rottenest luck. I'd have given my head to have gone with you.'

'I'm glad you didn't. It wasn't what you'd call a lady's tea-party.'

'Who wants a lady's tea-party? I ought to have gone in with the Mac Corps. Then I'd have had a chance.'

'Not this time. Mac draws the line somewhere. . . . Look here, Gwinnie, I wish you'd clear out a minute and let me talk to John.'

Gwinnie went, grumbling.

For a moment silence came down between

THE ROMANTIC

them. John was drinking coffee with an air of being alone in the room, pretending that he hadn't heard and didn't see her.

'John—I didn't mind driving that car. I knew I could do it, and I did it. I won't say I didn't mind the shelling, because I did. Still, shelling's all in the day's work. And I didn't mind your sending me, because I'd rather have gone myself than let you go. I don't want you to be killed. Somehow that's still the one thing I couldn't bear. But if you'd sent Gwinnie I'd have killed you.'

'I didn't send Gwinnie. I gave you your chance. I knew you wanted to cut Mrs Rankin out.'

'I? I never thought of such a rotten thing.'

'Well, you talked about danger as if you liked it.'

'So did you.'

'Oh—*go* to hell.'

'I've just come from there.'

'Oh—so you were frightened, were you?'

'Yes, I was horribly frightened. I had thirteen wounded men with me. What do you suppose it feels like, driving a heavy ambulance car by yourself? You can't sit in front and steer and look after thirteen wounded men at the same time. I had to keep hopping in and out. That isn't nice when there's shells about. I shall never forgive you for not coming to give a hand with those men. There's funk you can forgive, and——'

She thought: 'It's John—John—I'm saying these disgusting things to. I'm as bad as Trixie, telling him what I bloody well think of him, going back on him.'

'And there's funk——'

'You'd better take care, Charlotte. Do you know I could get you fired out of Belgium to-morrow?'

'Not after to-night, I think.' (It was horrible.)

He got up and opened the door. 'Anyhow, you'll clear out of this room now, damn you.'

'I wish you'd heard that Army doctor damning *you*.'

'Why didn't he go back with you himself, then?'

'*He* couldn't leave his wounded.'

He slammed the door hard behind her.

That was just like him. Wounded men everywhere, trying to sleep, and he slammed doors. He didn't care.

THE ROMANTIC

She would have to go on lying. She had made up her mind to that. So long as it would keep the others from knowing, so long as John's awfulness went beyond their knowledge, so long as it would do any good to John, she would lie.

Her time had come. She remembered saying that. She could hear herself talking to John at Barrow Hill Farm: 'Everybody's got their breaking point. . . . I dare say when my time comes I shall funk and lie.'

Well, didn't she? Funk—the everlasting funk of wondering what John would do next; and lying, lying at every turn to save him. *He* was her breaking point.

She had lied, the first time they went out, about the firing. She wondered whether she had done it because then, even then, she had been afraid of his fear. Hadn't she always somehow, in secret, been afraid? She could see the car coming round the corner by the church in the narrow street at Stow, she could feel it grazing her thigh, and John letting her go, jumping safe to the curb. She had pretended that it hadn't happened.

But that first day—no. He had been brave then. She had only lied because she was afraid he would worry about her. . . . Brave then.

JOHN RODEN CONWAY

Could war tire you and wear you down, and change you from yourself? In two weeks? Change him so that she had to hate him?

Half the night she lay awake wondering: Do I hate him because he doesn't care about me? Or because he doesn't care about the wounded? She could see all their faces: the face of the wounded man at Melle (*he* had crawled out on his hands and knees to look for her); the face of the dead boy who hadn't died when John left him; the Flamand they brought from Lokeren, lying in the road; the face of the dead man in the shed. And John's face.

How could you care for a thing like that? How could you want a thing like that to care for you?

And she? She didn't matter. Nothing mattered in all the world but Them.

XIV

It was Saturday, the tenth of October, the day after the fall of Antwerp. The Germans were pressing closer round Ghent; they might march in any day. She had been in Belgium a hundred years; she had lived a hundred years under this doom.

But at last she was free of John. Utterly free. His mind would have no power over her any more. Nor yet his body. She was glad that he had not been her lover. Supposing her body had been bound to him so that it couldn't get away? The struggle had been hard enough when her first flash came to her; and when she had fought against her knowledge and denied it, unable to face the truth that did violence to her passion; and when she had given him up and was left with just that, the beauty of his body, and it had hurt her to look at him.

Oh, well, nothing could hurt her now. And anyhow she would get through to-day without being afraid of what might happen. John couldn't do anything awful; he had been ordered on an absolutely safe expedition, taking medical stores to the convent hospital at Bruges and convoying Gurney, the sick chauffeur, to Ostend for England. Charlotte was to go out with Sutton, and Gwinnie was to take poor Gurney's place. She was glad she was going with Billy. Whatever happened Billy would go through it without caring, his mind fixed on the solid work.

And John, for an hour before he started, had been going about in gloom, talking of death. *His* death.

They were looking over the last letter from his father which he had asked her to answer for him. It seemed that John had told him the chances were he would be killed, and had asked him whether, in this case, he would allow the Roden ambulances to be handed over to McClane. And the old man had given his consent.

'Isn't it a pity to frighten him?' she said.

'He's no business to be frightened. It's *my* death. If I can face it, he can. I'm simply making necessary arrangements.'

She could see that. At the same time it struck her that he wanted you to see that he exposed

THE ROMANTIC

himself to all the risks of death, to see how he faced it. She had no patience with that talk about death; that pitiful bolstering up of his romance.

'If McClane says much more you can tell him.'

He was counting on this transfer of the ambulances to get credit with McClane; to silence him.

There were other letters which he had told her to answer. As soon as he had started she went into his room to look for them. If they were not on the chimneypiece they would be in the drawer with his razors and pocket-handkerchiefs.

It was John's room, after she had gone through it, that showed her what he was doing.

Sutton looked in before she had finished. She called to him, 'Billy, you might come here a minute.'

He came in, eyebrows lifted at the inquisition.

'What's up?'

'I'm afraid John isn't coming back.'

'Not coming back? Of course he's coming back.'

'No. I think he's—got off.'

'You mean he's———'

JOHN RODEN CONWAY

' Yes. Bolted.'

' What on earth makes you think that ? '

' He's taken all sorts of things—pyjamas, razors, all his pocket-handkerchiefs. . . . I *had* to look through his drawers to find those letters he told me to answer.'

Sutton had gone through into the slip of white-tiled lavatory beyond. She followed him.

' My God,' he said, ' Yes. He's taken his tooth-brush and his sleeping draught. . . . You know he tried to get leave yesterday and they wouldn't give it him ? '

' No. That makes it simply awful.'

' Pretty awful.'

' Billy—we must get him back.'

' I—I don't know about that. He isn't much good, is he ? I think we'd better let him go.'

' Don't you see how awful it'll be for the corps ? '

' The corps ? Does that matter ? McClane would take us all on to-morrow.'

' I mean for *us*. You and me and Gwinnie. He's our corps, and we're it.'

' Sharlie—with the Germans coming into Ghent do you honestly believe anybody'll remember what he did or didn't do ? '

' Yes. We're going to stick on with the

THE ROMANTIC

Belgian Army. It'll be remembered against *us*. Besides, it'll kill his father.'

'He'll do that anyway. He's rotten through and through.'

'No. He was splendid in the beginning. He might be splendid some day again. But if we let him go off and do this, he's done for.'

'He's done for anyhow. Isn't it better to recognise that he's rotten? McClane wouldn't have him. He saw what he was.'

'He didn't see him at Berlaere. He *was* splendid there.'

'My dear child, don't you know why? He didn't see there was any danger. He was too stupid to see it.'

'I saw it.'

'You're not stupid.'

'He did see it at the end.'

'At the end, yes—when he let you go back for the guns.'

She remembered. She remembered his face, the little beads of sweat glittering. He couldn't help that.

'Look here, from the time he realised the danger, did he go out or did he stay under cover?'

She didn't answer.

'There,' he said, 'you see.'

'Oh, Billy, won't you leave him one shred?'

'No. Not one shred.'

Yet, even now, if he could only be splendid—if he could only be it! Why shouldn't Billy leave him one shred? After all, he didn't know all the awful things John had done; and she would never tell him. . . . Her mind stood still. She remembered. . . . He did know two things, the two things she didn't know. She had got to know them. The desire that urged her to the completion of her knowledge pursued her now. She would possess him in her mind if in no other way.

'Billy—do you remember that day at Melle, when John lost me? Did you tell him I was going back with you?'

'No. I didn't.'

Then he *had* left her. And he had lied to both of them.

'Was the boy dead or alive when he left him?'

'He was alive all right. We could have saved him.'

He had died—he had died of fright, then.

'You *said* he was dead.'

'I know I did. I lied.'

THE ROMANTIC

'... And before that—when he was with you and Trixie on that battlefield—did he——'

'Yes. Then, too.... You see there aren't any shreds. The only thing you can say is he can't help it. Nobody'd have been hard on him if he hadn't gassed so much about danger.'

'That's the part you can't understand.... But, Billy, why did you lie about him?'

'Because I didn't want you to know then. I knew it would hurt you, I knew it would hurt you more than anything else.'

'That was rather wonderful of you.'

'Wasn't wonderful at all. I knew because what *you* think, what *you* feel, matters more to me than anything else. Except, perhaps, my job. I have to keep that separate.'

Her mind slid over that, not caring, returning to the object of its interest.

'Look here, Billy, you may be right. It probably doesn't matter to us. But it'll be perfectly awful for him.'

'They can't do anything to him, Sharlie.'

'It's what he'll do to himself.'

'Suicide? Not he.'

'I don't mean that. Can't you see that when he gets away to England, safe, and the funk settles down, he'll start romancing all over again.

He'll see the whole war again like that; and then he'll remember what he's done. He'll have to live all his life remembering. . . .'

'He won't. *You*'ll remember—*you*'ll suffer. You're feeling the shame he ought to feel and doesn't.'

'Well, somebody's got to feel it. . . . And he'll feel it too. He won't be let off. As long as he lives he'll remember. . . . I don't want him to have that suffering.'

'He's brought it on himself, Sharlie.'

'I don't care. I don't want him to have it. I couldn't bear it if he got away.'

'Of course, if you're going to be unhappy about it——'

'The only thing is, can we go after him? Can we spare a car?'

'Well, yes, I can manage that all right. The fact is, the Germans may really be in to-morrow or Monday, and we're thinking of evacuating all the British wounded to-day. There are some men here that we ought to take to Ostend. I've been talking to the President about it.'

And in the end they went with their wounded, less than an hour after John had started.

'I don't say I'll bring him back,' said Sutton. 'But, at any rate, we can find out what he's up

THE ROMANTIC

to.' He meditated. . . . 'We mayn't have to bring him. I shouldn't wonder if he came back on his own. He's like that. He can't stand danger yet he keeps on coming back to it. Can't leave it alone.'

'I know. He isn't quite an ordinary coward.'

'I'm not sure. I've known chaps like that. Can't keep away from the thing.'

But she stuck to it. John's cowardice was not like other people's cowardice. Other cowards going into danger had the imagination of horror. He had nothing but the imagination of romantic delight. It was the reality that became too much for him. He was either too stupid, or too securely wrapped up in his dream to reckon with reality. It surprised him every time. And he had no imaginative fear of fear. His fear must have surprised him.

'He'll have got away from Bruges,' she said.

'I don't think so. He'll have to put up at the convent for a bit, to let Gurney rest.'

They had missed the convent and were running down a narrow street towards the Market Place when they found John. He came on across a white bridge over a canal at the bottom. He was escorted by some Belgian women, dressed in black; they were talking and pointing up the street.

He said he had been to lunch in the town and had lost himself there, and they were showing him the way back to the convent.

She had seen all that before somewhere, John coming over the canal bridge with the women in black. . . . She remembered. That was in one of her three dreams. Only what she saw now was incomplete. There had been something more in the dream. Something had happened.

It happened half an hour later when she went out to find John in the convent garden where he was walking with the nuns. The garden shimmered in a silver mist from the canal, the broad grass plots, the clipped hedges, the cones and spikes of yew, the tall, feathery chrysanthemums, the trailing bowers and arches, were netted and laced and webbed with the silver mist. Down at the bottom of the path the forms of John and the three women showed blurred and insubstantial and still.

Presently they emerged, solid and clear; the nuns in their black habits and the raking white caps like wings that set them sailing along. They

THE ROMANTIC

were showing John their garden, taking a shy, gentle, absorbed possession of him.

And as she came towards him John passed her without speaking. But his face had turned to her with the look she had seen before. Eyes of hatred, eyes that repudiated and betrayed her.

The nuns had stopped, courteously, to greet her; she fell behind with one of them; the two others had overtaken John, who had walked on, keeping up his stiff, repudiating air.

The air, the turn of the head, the look that she had dreamed. Only in the dream it had hurt her, and now she was hard and had no pain.

It was in the convent garden that they played it out, in one final, astounding conversation.

The nuns had brought two chairs on to the flagged terrace and set a small table there covered with a white cloth. Thus invited, John had no choice but to take his place beside her. Still he retained his mood.

(The nuns left them. Sutton was in one of the wards, helping with an operation.)

'I thought,' he said, 'that I was going to have peace. . . .'

JOHN RODEN CONWAY

It seemed to her that they had peace. They had been so much at the mercy of chance moments that this secure hour given to them in the closed garden seemed, in its quietness, immense.

'. . . But first it's Sutton, then it's you.'

'We needn't say anything unless you like. There isn't much to be said.'

'Oh, isn't there!'

'Not,' she said, 'if you're coming back.'

'Of course I'm coming back. . . . Look here, Charlotte. You didn't suppose I was really going to bolt, did you?'

'Were you going to change into your pyjamas at Ostend?'

'My pyjamas? I brought them for Gurney.'

'And your sleeping draught was for Gurney?'

'Of course it was.'

'And your razors and your tooth-brush too. Oh, John, what's the good of lying? You forget that I helped Alice Bartrum to pack Gurney's things. You forget that Billy knows.'

'Do I? I shan't forget your going back on me; your betraying me,' he said.

THE ROMANTIC

And for the first time she realised how alone he was; how horribly alone. He had nobody but her.

'Who have I betrayed you to?'

'To Sutton. To McClane. To everybody you talked to.'

'No. No.'

'Yes. And you betrayed me in your thoughts. That's worse. People don't always mean what they say. It's what they think.'

'What was I to think?'

'Why, that all the damnable things you said about me weren't true.'

'I didn't say anything.'

'You've betrayed me by the things you didn't say.'

'Why should I have betrayed you?'

'You know why. When a woman betrays a man it's always for one reason.

He threw his head back to strike at her with his eyes, hard and keen, dark blue like the blade of a new knife. . . . 'Because he hasn't given her what she wants.'

'Oh, what I want—I thought we'd settled that long ago.'

'You've never settled it. It isn't in you to settle it.'

JOHN RODEN CONWAY

'I can't talk to you about that. You're too horrible. But I didn't betray you.'

'You listened to people who betrayed me. If you cared for me in any decent way you'd have stood by me.'

'I *have* stood by you through thick and thin. I've lied your lies. There isn't one of your lies I haven't backed. I've done everything I could think of to keep people from knowing about you.'

'Yet you go and tell Sutton that I've bolted. That I'm a deserter.'

'Yes, when it was all over. If you'd got away everybody'd have known. As it is, only Billy and I know; and he's safe.'

'You insist that I was trying to get away? I own I thought of it. But one doesn't do everything one thinks of. . . . No. . . . Don't imagine I was sick of the war, or sick of Belgium. It's you I'm sick of.'

'Me?'

'Yes, you. You had your warning. I told you what would happen if you let me see you wanted me.'

'You think you've seen that?'

'I've seen nothing else.'

'Once, perhaps. Twice. Once when you

came to me on Barrow Hill. And when we were crossing once. And each time you never saw it.'

'Anybody can see. It's in your face. In your eyes and mouth. You can't hide your lust.'

'My—"lust." Don't you know I only cared for you because I'd done with that?'

They stopped. The nuns were back again, bringing great cups of hot black coffee, coming quietly, and going quietly away. It was wonderful, all that beauty and gentleness and peace existing in the horror of the war, and through this horror within horror that John had made.

They drank their coffee, slowly, greedily, prolonging this distraction from their torment. Charlotte finished first.

'You say I want you. I own I did once. But I don't now. Why, I care more for the scrubbiest little Belgian with a smashed finger than I do for you.'

'I suppose you can satisfy your erotic susceptibilities that way.'

'I haven't any, I tell you. I only cared for you because I thought you were clean. I thought your mind was beautiful. And you aren't clean. And your mind's the ugliest thing I know. And the cruellest. . . . Let's get it right, John. I can forgive your funking. If your nerves are jumpy they are jumpy. I dare say *I* shall be jumpy if the Germans come into Ghent before I'm out of it. I can forgive everything you've done to *me*. I can forgive your lying. I see there's nothing left for you but to lie. . . . But I can't forgive your not caring for the wounded. That's cruel. . . . You didn't care for that boy at Melle——'

John's mouth opened as if he were going to say something. He seemed to gasp.

'——No, you didn't or you wouldn't have left him. Whatever your funk was like, you couldn't have left him if you'd cared, any more than I could have left *you*.'

'He was dead when I left him.'

'He was still warm when I found him. Billy thought you were bringing him away. He says he wasn't dead.'

'He lies, then. But you'll take his word against mine.'

'Yes,' she said simply. 'And he says he *didn't* tell you I was going on with him. You don't care for *me*. If you'd cared you couldn't have left me.'

'I thought you said if it was a toss up

THE ROMANTIC

between you and a wounded man——? There were wounded men in that car.'

'There was a wounded man with me. You left *him*. . . . Don't imagine I cared about myself, whether I lived or died. It was because I cared about you. I cared so awfully.'

He jerked out a laugh. One light, short sound of dismissal and contempt.

XV

That light sound he made had ended it.

She remembered it afterwards, not as a thing that hurt her, but as an unpleasant incident of the day, like the rudeness of a stranger, and yet not to be forgotten. It had the importance of extreme finality; his answer to everything, unanswerable.

She didn't care. She had ended it herself and with so clean a cut that she could afford to let him have that inarticulate last word. She had left him nothing to do but keep up his pretence that there had never been so much as a beginning. He gave no sign of anything having been between them, unless his attitude to Sutton was a sign.

It showed the next day, the terrible Sunday that was ending everything. Yesterday he had given orders that Charlotte should drive Sutton while he drove by himself. To-day he had changed all that. Gwinnie was to drive Sutton and Charlotte was to go out alone. And he had offered himself to McClane. To McClane.

THE ROMANTIC

That gave her the measure of his resentment. She could see that he coupled her with Sutton while he yet tried to keep them apart. He was not going to have more to do with either of them than he could help.

So that she had hardly seen or heard of him that day. And when the solid work began she found that she could turn him out of her mind as if he had never been there. The intolerable burden of him slipped from her; all morning she had a sense of cold clearness and lightness; and she judged that her deliverance was complete.

She had waited a long time with her car drawn up close under the house wall in the long street at Melle. McClane's car stood in front of her, waiting for John. He was up there on the battlefield, with Sutton and McClane. McClane had kept him off it all day; he had come to her when they started and told her not to worry. Conway would be all right. He would see that he didn't get into places where he—well, unsuitable places. He would keep him driving. But in the end one of the stretcher-bearers had given in, and John had to take his turn.

He had been keen to go. Keen. She could see him swinging along up the road to the

JOHN RODEN CONWAY

battlefield and McClane with him, running to keep up with his tall stride.

She had taken her turn too, and she knew what it was like up there. Endless turnip fields; turnips thrown up as if they had been pulled, livid roots that rotted, and the wounded and the dead men lying out among them. You went stumbling; the turnips rolled and slipped under your feet. Seeing things.

Her mind looked the other way, frightened. She was tired out, finished; she could have gone to sleep now, sitting up there on the car. It would be disgraceful if she went to sleep. . . .

She mustn't think about the battlefield. She couldn't think; she could only look on at things coming up in her mind. Hoeing turnips at Barrow Hill Farm. Supposing you found dead men lying out on the fields at Stow? You would mind that more; it would be more horrible. . . . She saw herself coming over the fields carrying a lamb that she had taken from its dead mother. Then she saw John coming up the field to their seat in the beech ring. *That* hurt her; she couldn't bear it; she mustn't think about that.

John was all right; he wasn't shirking. They had been away so long now that she knew they

THE ROMANTIC

must have gone far down the battlefield, deep into it; the edges and all the nearer places had been gleaned. It would be dark before they came back.

It was getting dark now, and she was afraid that when the light went she would go to sleep. If only she wasn't so tired.

She was so drowsy that at first she didn't hear McClane speaking, she hadn't seen him come to the step of the car.

McClane's voice sounded soft and unnatural and a little mysterious.

'I'm afraid something's—happened.'

'Who to?'

'We-ell——'

The muffled drawl irritated her. Why couldn't he speak out?

'Is John hurt?'

'I'm afraid so.'

'Is he killed?'

'Well—I don't know that he can live. A German's put a bullet into him.'

'Where is he?'

She jumped down off the car.

McClane laid his hand on her arm. 'Don't. We shall bring him in——'

'He's dead, then?'

JOHN RODEN CONWAY

'I think so—you'd better not go to him.'

'Of course I'm going to him. Where *is* he?'

He steered her very quickly and carefully across the street, then led her with his arm in hers, pressing her back to the dark shelter of the houses. They heard the barking of machine guns from the battlefield at the top and the rattle of the bullets on the causeway. These sounds seemed to her to have no significance. As if they had existed only in some unique relation to John Conway, his death robbed them of vitality.

The door of the house opened a little way; they slipped into the long, narrow room, lighted by a few oil lamps at one end. At the other John's body lay on a stretcher set up on a trestle table, his feet turned outwards to the door, ready. The corners at this end were so dark that the body seemed to stretch across the whole width of the room. A soldier came forward with a lighted candle and gave it to McClane. And she saw John's face; the bridge of his nose, with its winged nostrils lifted. His head was tilted upwards at the chin; that gave it a noble look. His mouth was open, ever so slightly open. . . . McClane shifted the light so that it fell on his forehead. . . . Black eyebrows curling

THE ROMANTIC

up like little moustaches. . . . The half-dropped eyelids guarded the dead eyes.

She thought of how he used to dream. All his dream was in his dead face; his dead face was cold and beautiful, like his dream.

As she looked at him her breast closed down on her heart as though it would never lift again; her breath shuddered there under her tightened throat. She could feel McClane's hand pressing heavily on her shoulder. She had no strength to shake it off; she was even glad of it. She felt small and weak and afraid; afraid, not of the beautiful thing that lay there, but of something terrible and secret that it hid, something that any minute she would have to know about.

'Where was he hit?'

'In the back.'

She trembled, and McClane's hand pressed closer. 'The bullet passed clean through his heart. He didn't suffer.'

'He was getting in Germans?'

'I don't—quite—know'—McClane measured his words out one by one—'what—he was doing. Sutton was with him. He knows.'

'Where *is* Billy?'

'Over there. Do you want him?'

'Not yet.'

JOHN RODEN CONWAY

A soldier brought a chair for her. She sat down with her back to the trestle table. At the lighted end of the room she saw Sutton stooping over a young Belgian captain, buttoning his tunic under the sling he had adjusted. The captain's face showed pure and handsome, like a girl's, like a young nun's, bound round and chin-wrapped in the white bandages. He sat on the floor in front of Sutton's table with his legs stretched out flat. His back was propped against the thigh of a Belgian soldier seated on an upturned barrel. Her hurt eyes saw them very plain and with detail in the light of Sutton's lamp.

That part of the room was full of soldiers. She noticed that they kept clear of the trestle table as they went in and out. Only one of them, the soldier who supported the young captain, kept on looking, raising his head and looking there as if he couldn't turn his eyes away. He faced her. His rifle stood steadied by his knees, the bayonet pointing up between his eyes.

She found herself thinking. It was Sutton's back that made her think. John must have been stooping over the German like that. John's wound was in his back. But if he was stooping

THE ROMANTIC

it couldn't have come that way. The bullet would have gone through his chest. . . . Perhaps he had turned to pick up his stretcher. Billy was there. He would tell her how it had happened.

She thought: No. I've had enough. I shall give it up. I won't ask him. But she knew that she would ask him. Once started, having gone so far, flash by flash and step by step, she couldn't give it up; she would go on, even now, till her knowledge was complete. Then she was aware again of the soldier's eyes.

They were very large and bright and black in his smooth boy's face; he had a small innocent boy's mouth that seemed to move, restless and fascinated, like his eyes. Presently she saw that he was looking at her, that his eyes returned to her again and again, as if he were aware of some connection between her and the thing that fascinated him, as if *he* were somehow connected.

He was listening to her now as Sutton spoke to her.

'We must get him away quick.'

'Yes. Do let's get him away.'

Sutton shook his head. He was thinking of the wounded captain.

'We can't yet. I'll come back for him.'

JOHN RODEN CONWAY

'Then I'll wait with him here.'

'Oh, no—I think——'

'I can't leave him.'

'It isn't safe. The place may be taken.'

'I won't leave him.' Sutton hesitated. 'I won't, Billy.'

'McClane, she says she won't leave him.'

'Then,' McClane said, 'we must take him now. We'll have to make room somehow.'

(To make room for him—somehow.)

Sutton and the soldier carried the captain out and came back for John's body. The Belgian sprang forward with eager, subservient alacrity to put himself at the head of the stretcher, but Sutton thrust him aside.

The Belgian shrugged his shoulders and picked up his rifle with an air of exaggerated unconcern. Sutton and McClane carried out the stretcher.

Charlotte was following them when the soldier stopped her.

'Mademoiselle——'

He had propped his rifle against the trestles and stood there, groping in his pocket. A dirty handkerchief, dragged up by his fumbling, hung out by its corner. All along the sharp crease there was a slender smear of blood. He looked down at it and pushed it back out of her sight.

THE ROMANTIC

He had taken something out of his pocket.

'I will give you this. I found it on the battlefield.'

He handed her a small leather pocket-book that was John's. It had her photograph in it, and his, taken together.

They were putting him out of sight, under the hood of the ambulance, and she waited there when the war correspondent came up.

'*Can* you tell me the name of the volunteer who's been killed?'

'Conway. John Roden Conway.'

'What? *That* man? The man who raced the Germans into Zele?'

'Yes,' she said. 'That man.'

She was in John's room, packing, gathering together the things she would have to take to his father. Sutton came to her there.

They had orders to be ready for the retreat any time that night.

Billy had brought her John's wrist-watch and cigarette-case.

'Billy,' she said, 'that soldier gave me this.'

She showed him the pocket-book.

'What soldier?'

'The one who was with the captain.'

JOHN RODEN CONWAY

'*He* gave it you?'

'Yes. He said he found it on the battlefield. It must have dropped out of John's pocket.'

'It couldn't have dropped. . . . I wonder why he kept that.'

'But he didn't keep it. He gave it to me.'

'He was going to keep it, or he'd have handed it over to me with the other things.'

'Does it matter?'

'Well——'

She thought: Why can't he leave it alone? They *had* all his things, his poor things.

But Sutton was still thoughtful. 'I wonder why he gave it you.'

'I think he was sorry.'

'*Was* he?'

'Sorry for me, I mean.'

Sutton said nothing. He was absorbed in contemplating the photograph. They had been taken standing by the hurdle of the sheepfold, she with the young lamb in her arms and John looking down at her.

'That was taken at Barrow Hill Farm,' she said, 'where we were together. He looked just like that. . . . Oh, Billy, do you think the past's really past? . . . Isn't there some way he could go on being what he *was*?'

THE ROMANTIC

'I don't know, Sharlie, I don't know.'

'Why couldn't he have stayed there? Then he'd always have been like that. We should never have known.'

'You're not going to be unhappy about him?'

'No. I think I'm glad. It's a sort of relief. I shan't ever have that awful feeling of wondering what he'll do next. . . . Billy—you were with him, weren't you?'

'Yes.'

'Was he all right?'

'Would it make you happier to think he was or to know he wasn't?'

'Oh—just to *know*.'

'Well, I'm afraid he wasn't, quite. . . . He paid for it, Sharlie. If he hadn't turned his back he wouldn't have been shot.'

She nodded.

'What? You knew?'

'No. No. I wasn't sure.'

She was possessed by this craving to know, to know everything. Short of that she would be still bound to him; she could never get free.

'Billy—what did happen, really? Did he *leave* the German?'

'The German?'

'Yes. Was that why he shot him?'

JOHN RODEN CONWAY

'The German didn't shoot him. He was too far gone, poor devil, to shoot anybody. . . . It was the Belgian captain that he left. . . . He was lying there, horribly wounded. His servant was with him; they were calling out to Conway——'

'*Calling* to him?'

'Yes. And he was going all right when some shrapnel fell—a regular shower-bath, quite near, like it did with you and me. That scared him and he just turned and ran. The servant shouted to him to stop, and when he wouldn't he went after him and put a bullet through his back.'

'That Belgian boy?'

'Yes. I couldn't do anything. I had the German. It was all over in a second. . . . When I got there I found the Belgian standing up over him, wiping his bayonet with his pocket-handkerchief. He *said* his rifle went off by accident.'

'Couldn't it? Rifles do.'

'Bayonets don't. . . . I suppose I could get him court-martialled if I tried. But I shan't. After all, it was his captain. I don't blame him, Charlotte.'

'No. . . . It was really you and me, Billy. We brought him back to be killed.'

THE ROMANTIC

'I don't know that we did bring him—that he wasn't coming by himself. He couldn't keep off it. Even if we did, you wouldn't be sorry for that, would you?'

'No. It was the best thing we could do for him.'

'Yes, we gave him his chance.'

But at night, lying awake in her bed, she cried. For then she remembered what he had been. On Barrow Hill, on their seat in the beech ring, through the Sunday evenings, when feeding time and milking time were done.

At four o'clock in the morning she was waked by Sutton, standing beside her bed. The orders had come through to evacuate the hospital. Three hours later the ambulances had joined the great retreat.

XVI

They had halted in Bruges, and there their wounded had been taken into the convent wards to rest.

Charlotte and Sutton were sitting out, alone together, on the flagged terrace in the closed garden. The nuns had brought out the two chairs again, and set again the little table covered with the white cloth. Again the silver mist was in the garden, but thinned now to the clearness of still water.

They had been silent after the nuns had left them. Sutton's sad, short-sighted eyes stared out at the garden without seeing it. He was lost in melancholy. Presently he came to himself with a long sigh——

'Charlotte, what are we going to do now? Do you know?'

'*I* know. I'm going into Mac's corps.'

'So am I. That isn't what I meant.'

For a moment she didn't stop to wonder what

THE ROMANTIC

he did mean. She was too full of what she was going to do.

'Is that wise? I don't altogether trust old Mac. He'll use you till you drop. He'll wear you to the last shred of your nerves.'

'I want to be used till I drop. I want to be worn. Besides, I know I'm safe with Mac.'

His cold, hard indifference made her feel safe. She wasn't really safe with Billy. His goodness might disarm her any minute, his sadness might conceivably move her to a tender weakness. But for McClane she would never have any personal feeling, never any fiery affection, any exalted devotion. Neither need she be afraid of any profound betrayal. Small betrayals, perhaps, superficial disasters to her vanity, while his egoism rode over it in triumph. He didn't want affection or anything fiery, anything that John had had. He would leave her in her hardness; he would never ask anything but hard, steel-cold loyalty and a willingness to share his risks.

'What else can I do? I should have come out if John hadn't. Of course I was glad we could go together, but you mustn't suppose I only went because of him.'

JOHN RODEN CONWAY

'I don't. I only thought perhaps you wouldn't want to stay on now he's dead.'

'More than ever now he's dead. Even if I didn't want to stay I should have to now. To make up.'

'For what?'

'For what he did. All those awful things. And for what he didn't do. His dreams. I've got to do what he dreamed. But more than anything I must pay his debt to Belgium. To all those wounded men.'

'You're not responsible for his debts, Charlotte.'

'No? Sometimes I feel as if I were. As if he and I were tied up together. I could get away from him when he was alive. But now he's dead he's got me.'

'It doesn't make him different.'

'It makes *me* different. I tell you, I can't get away from him. And I want to. I want to cut myself loose; and this is the way.'

'Isn't it the way to tie yourself tighter?'

'No. Not when it's *done*, Billy.'

'I can see a much better way. .... If you married me.'

She turned to him, astonished and a little

THE ROMANTIC

anxious, as though she thought something odd and dangerous had happened to him.

'Oh, Billy, I—I couldn't do that. . . . What made you think of it?'

'I've been thinking of it all the time.'

'All the time?'

'Well, most of the time, anyhow. But I've loved you all the time. You know I loved you. That was why I stuck to Conway. I couldn't leave you to him. I wouldn't even leave you to McClane.'

'I didn't know.'

'I should have thought it was pretty obvious.'

'It wasn't. I'd have tried to stop it if I'd known.'

'You couldn't have stopped it.'

'I'm sorry.'

'What about?'

'That. It isn't any good. It really isn't.'

'Why isn't it? I know I'm rather a queer chap. And I've got an ugly face——'

'I love your *face*. . . .'

She loved it, with its composure and its candour, its slightly flattened features, laid back; its little surprised moustache, its short-sighted eyes, and its sadness.

JOHN RODEN CONWAY

'It's the dearest face. But——'

'I suppose,' he said, 'it sounds a bit startling and sudden. But if you'd been bottling it up as long as I have—why, I loved you the first time I saw you. On the boat. . . . So you see, it's you. It isn't just anything you've done.'

'If you knew what I *have* done, my dear. If you only knew. You wouldn't want to marry me.'

She would have to tell him. That would put him off. That would stop him. If she had loved him she would have had to tell him, as she had told John.

'I'm going to tell you. . . .'

. . . . . .

She wondered whether he had really listened. A queer smile played about his mouth. He looked as if he had been thinking of something else all the time.

'What are you smiling at?'

'Your supposing that that would make any difference.'

'Doesn't it?'

'Not a bit. Not a little bit. . . . Besides, I knew it.'

'Who—who told you?'

THE ROMANTIC

'The only other person who knew about it, I suppose—Conway.'

'He betrayed me?'

'He betrayed you. Is there any vile thing he didn't do?'

And it was as it had been before. The nuns came out again, bringing the great cups of hot black coffee, coming and going gently. Only this time she couldn't drink.

'It's awful of us,' she said, ' to talk about him this way when he's dead.'

'He isn't dead as long as he makes you feel like that. As long as he keeps you from me.'

A long pause. And then, ' Billy—he wasn't my lover.'

'I know that,' he said fiercely. 'He took good care to tell me.'

'I brought it all on myself. I ought to have given him up instead of hanging on to him that way. Platonic love—it's all wrong. People aren't really made like that. It was every bit as bad as going to Gibson Herbert. . . . Worse. That was honest. This was all lying. Lying about myself. Lying about him. Lying about —love.'

JOHN RODEN CONWAY

'Then,' he said, 'you don't really know what it is.'

'I know John's sort. And I know Gibson's sort. And I know there's a heavenly sort, Billy, in between. But I'm spoiled for it. I think I could have cared for you if it hadn't been for John. . . . I shan't ever get away from him.'

'Yes. If you can see it——'

'Of course I see it. I can see everything now. All that war-romancing. I see how awful it was. When I think how we went out and got thrills. Fancy getting thrills out of this horror.'

'Oh, well—I think you earned your thrill.'

'You can't earn anything in this war. At least *I* can't. It's paying, paying all the time. And I've got more things than John to pay for. There was little Effie.'

'Effie?'

'Gibson's wife. I didn't *want* to hurt her. . . . Billy, are you sure it makes no difference? What I did.'

'I've told you it doesn't. . . . You mustn't go on thinking about it.'

'No. But I can't get over his betraying me. You see, that's the worst thing he did to *me*.

THE ROMANTIC

The other things—well, he was mad with fright, and he was afraid of me, because I knew. I can't think why he did this.'

'Same reason. You knew. He was degraded by your knowledge, so you had to be degraded. At least I suppose that's how it was.'

She shook her head. He was darker to her than ever and she was no nearer to her peace. She knew everything and she understood nothing. And that was worse than not knowing.

'If only I could understand. Then, I believe, I could bear it. I wouldn't care how bad it was as long as I understood.'

'Ask McClane then. He could explain it to you. It's beyond me.'

'McClane?'

'He's a psychotherapist. He knows more about people's souls than I know about their bodies. He probably knows all about Conway's soul.'

Silence drifted between them, dim and silvery like the garden mist.

'Charlotte—are we never to get away from him? Is he always to stick between us? That dead man.'

'It isn't that.'

JOHN RODEN CONWAY

' What is it, then ? '

' All *this*. .... I'd give anything to care for you, Billy dear, but I don't care. I *can't*. I can't care for anything but the war.'

' The war won't last for ever. And afterwards ? '

' I can't see any afterwards.'

Sutton smiled.

' And yet,' he said, ' there will be one.'

XVII

THE boat went steadily, cutting the waves with its sound like the flowing of stiff silk.

Charlotte and Sutton and McClane, stranded at Dunkirk on their way to England, had been taken on board the naval transport, *Victoria*. They were the only passengers besides some young soldiers, and these had left them a clear space on the deck. Charlotte was sitting by herself under the lee of a cabin when McClane came to her there.

He was straddling and rubbing his hands. Something had pleased him.

'I knew,' he said, 'that some day I should get you three. And that I should get those ambulances.'

She couldn't tell whether he meant that he always got what he wanted or that he had foreseen John Conway's fate which would ultimately give it him.

'The ambulances—yes. You always wanted them.'

JOHN RODEN CONWAY

'Not more than I wanted you and Sutton.'

He seemed aware of her secret antagonism, yet without resentment, waiting till it had died down before he spoke again. He was sitting beside her now.

'What are you going to do about Conway?'

'Nothing. Except lie about him to his father.'

'That all right, as long as you don't lie about him to yourself.'

'I've lied about him to other people. Never to myself. I was in love with him, if that's what you mean. But he finished that. What's finished is finished. I haven't a scrap of feeling for him left.'

'Are you quite sure?'

'Quite. I'm not even sorry he's dead.'

'You've forgiven him?'

'I'm not always sure about that. But I'm trying to forget him.'

McClane looked away.

'Do you ever dream about him, Charlotte?'

'Never. Not now. I used to. I dreamed about him once three nights running.'

He looked at her sharply. 'Could you tell me what you dreamed?'

She told him her three dreams.

THE ROMANTIC

' You don't suppose they meant anything ? ' she said.

' I do. They meant that part of you was kicking. It knew all the time what he was like and was trying to warn you.'

' To keep me off him ? '

' To keep you off him.'

' I see. . . . The middle one was funny. It *happened*. The day we were in Bruges. But I can't make out the first one with that awful woman in it.'

' You may have been dreaming something out of his past. Something he remembered.'

' Well, anyhow, I don't understand the last one.'

' I do.'

' But I dreamed he wanted me. Frightfully. And he didn't.'

' He did. He wanted you—" frightfully "—all the time. He went to pieces if you weren't there. Don't you know why he took you out with him everywhere ? Because if he hadn't he couldn't have driven half a mile out of Ghent.'

' That's one of the things I'm trying to forget.'

' It's one of the things you should try to remember.'

He grasped her arm.

'And, Charlotte, look here. I want you to forgive him. For your own sake.'

She stiffened under his touch, his look, his voice of firm, intimate authority. His insincerity repelled her.

'Why should you? You don't care about him. You don't care about me. If I was blown to bits to-morrow you wouldn't care.'

He laughed his mirthless, assenting laugh.

'You don't care about people at all. You only care about their diseases and their minds and things.'

'I think I care a little about the wounded.'

'You don't really. Not about *them*. You care about getting in more of them and quicker than any other field ambulance on the front. I can't think why you're bothering about me now.'

'That's why. If I'm to get in more wounded I can't have anybody in my corps who isn't fit.'

'*I'm* fit. What's the matter with me?'

'Not much. Your body's all right. And your mind *was* all right till Conway upset it. Now it's unbalanced.'

'Unbalanced?'

THE ROMANTIC

'Just the least little bit. There's a fight going on in it between your feeling for Conway and your knowledge of him.'

'I've told you I haven't any feeling.'

'Your memory of your feeling then. Same thing. You know he was cruel and a liar and a coward. And you loved him. With you those two states are incompatible. They struggle. And that's bad for you. If it goes on you'll break down. If it stops you'll be all right. . . . The way to stop it is to know the *truth* about Conway. The truth won't clash with your feeling.'

'Don't I know it?'

'Not all. Not the part that matters most. You know he was all wrong morally. You don't know *why*. . . . Conway was an out and out degenerate. He couldn't help *that*. He suffered from some physical disability. It went through everything. It made him so that he couldn't live a man's life. He was afraid to enter a profession. He was afraid of women.'

'He wasn't afraid of me. Not in the beginning.'

'Because he felt your strength. You're very strong, Charlotte. You gave him your strength. And he could *feel* passion, mind you, though he couldn't act it. . . . I suppose he could feel courage too, only, somehow, he couldn't make it work. Have you got it clear?'

She nodded. So clear that it seemed to her he was talking about a thing she had known once and had forgotten. All the time she had known John's secret. She knew what would come next: McClane's voice saying, 'Well, then, think—think,' and his excited gestures, bobbing forward suddenly from the hips. He went on.

'The balance had to be righted somehow. His whole life must have been a struggle to right it. Unconscious, of course. Instinctive. His platonics were just a glorifying of his disability. All that romancing was a gorgeous transformation of his funk. . . . So that his very lying was a sort of truth. I mean it was part of the whole desperate effort after completion. He jumped at everything that helped him to get compensation, to get power. He jumped at your feeling for him because it gave him power. He jumped at the war because the thrill he got out of it gave him the sense of power. He sucked manhood out of you. He sucked it out of everything—out of blood and wounds. . . . He'd have been faithful to you for ever, Charlotte, if you hadn't found him out. *That* upset all his delicate

THE ROMANTIC

adjustments. The war upset him. I think the sight of blood and wounds whipped up the naked savage in him.'

'But—no. He was afraid of that.'

'He was afraid of himself. Of what was in him. That fear of his was his protection, like his fear of women. The war broke it down. Then he was cruel to you.'

'Yes. He was cruel.' Her voice sounded flat and hard, without feeling. She had no feeling; she had exhausted all the emotions of her suffering. And her knowledge of his cruelty was absolute. To McClane's assertion of the fact she had no response beyond that toneless acquiescence.

'Taking you into that shed——'

He had roused her.

'How on earth did you know that? I've never told a single soul.'

'It was known in the hospital. One of the carpenters saw the whole thing. He told one of our orderlies, who told my chauffeur, Gurney, who told me.'

'It doesn't matter what he did to *me*. I can't get over his not caring for the wounded.'

'He was jealous of them, because you cared for them.'

'Oh, no. He'd left off caring for me by then.'

JOHN RODEN CONWAY

'*Had* he?' He gave a little soft, wise laugh. 'What makes you think so?'

'That. His cruelty.'

'Love can be very cruel.'

'Not as cruel as that,' she said.

'Yes. As cruel as that. . . . Remember, it was at the bottom of the whole business. Of his dreams. In a sense, the real John Conway was the man who dreamed.'

'If you're right he was the man who was cruel, too. And it's his cruelty I hate.'

'Don't hate it. Don't hate it. I want you to understand his cruelty. It wasn't just savagery. It was something subtler. A supreme effort to get power. Remember, he couldn't help it. He *had* to right himself. Supposing his funk extinguished something in him that could only be revived through cruelty? You'll say he could help betraying you——'

'To you, too?'

'To me, too. When you lost faith in him you cut off his main source of power. You had to be discredited so that it shouldn't count. You mustn't imagine that he did anything on purpose. He was driven. It sounds horrible, but I want you to see it was just his way of saving his soul, the only way open to him. You mustn't think of it as a bad way. Or a good way. It wasn't even *his* way. It was the way of something bigger than he was, bigger than anything he could ever be. Bigger than badness or goodness.'

'Did "it" do cowardly things to "save" itself?'

'No. If Conway could have played the man "it" would have been satisfied. It was always urging him. . . . Try,' he said, and she knew that now at any rate he was sincere; he really wanted to help her; he was giving her his best. His voice was very quiet now, his excited gestures had ceased. 'Try to think of it as something more real, more important and necessary than he was; or you and I. Something that is always struggling to be, to go on being. Something that degeneracy is always trying to keep under. . . . Power. A power in retreat, fighting to get back its lost ground.'

Then what she had loved was not John Conway. What she had hated was not he. He was this Something, tremendous and necessary, that escaped your judgment. You couldn't hurt it with your loving or hating or your ceasing to love and hate. Something that tortured you and betrayed you because that was the only way it knew to save itself.

JOHN RODEN CONWAY

Something that couldn't save itself altogether—that clung to you and called to you to save it.

But that *was* what she had loved. Nothing could touch it.

For a moment while McClane was talking, she saw, in the flash he gave her, that it was real. And when the flash went it slipped back into her darkness.

But on the deck in front of her she could see John walking up and down. She could see the wide road of gold and purple that stretched from the boat's stern to the sun. John's head was thrown back; he looked at her with his shining, adventurous eyes. He was happy and excited, going out to the war.

And she saw them again: the batteries, the cars, and the wagons. Dust like blown smoke, and passing in it the long lines of beaten men, reeling slowly to the footway, passing slowly, endlessly, regiment by regiment, in retreat.

GLASGOW: W. COLLINS SONS AND CO. LTD.

A few of COLLINS' Latest Books

Messrs COLLINS will always be glad to send particulars regularly to readers who will supply their names and addresses

HARVEST

By Mrs Humphry Ward

Author of *Cousin Philip*, etc.

SECOND IMPRESSION.   7s. 6d. net

'A strong, skilfully told tale.'—*Times*.

'Well sustained from beginning to end, and the pathetic figure of Rachel makes a strong appeal to the reader.'—*Daily Telegraph*.

'Admirably characteristic of its writer's great and undimmed qualities, and one which brings the tale of her achievement to a worthy and congruous close.'—*Westminster Gazette*.

'Perhaps the simplest Mrs Ward ever wrote, and on that account one of the best.'—*Morning Post*.

Recent Publications

THE TALL VILLA
By Lucas Malet
Author of *Sir Richard Calmady, Deadham Hard*, etc.   7s. 6d. *net*

'Close on an impeccable novel. The characters are beautifully balanced . . . the style is admirable—excellently written.'—*Times*.

'Takes rank with the finest. It is exquisitely told, and is probably Lucas Malet's greatest achievement . . . related with a delicate and subtle charm there is no resisting.'—*Pall Mall Gazette*.

'Told with a subtlety of suggestion which makes it curiously arresting . . . told with beautiful art.'—*Scotsman*.

'A haunting little tale of a ghostly visitation told with exquisite delicacy and restraint . . . superbly told . . . a gem.'—*Daily Chronicle*.

AN IMPERFECT MOTHER
By J. D. Beresford
Author of *God's Counterpoint, Jacob Stahl*, etc.
THIRD IMPRESSION.   7s. 6d. *net*

'A highly entertaining example of pure intellect . . . which, for my own part, I enjoyed amazingly.'—*Punch*.

'Takes his reader in the delicate but firm grip proper to an accomplished novelist entering into his subject with two of the most delightful opening chapters he has ever written . . . Mr Beresford at his best.'—*Westminster Gazette*.

Recent Publications

DENYS THE DREAMER
By Katharine Tynan
Author of *The Man from Australia*, etc.

7s. 6d. net

'The writer, so long and so widely admired by her readers under her maiden name of Katharine Tynan, was happy far beyond the common in delineating the best aspects of Irish character. Her novel is a typical and charming example of her talent . . . and the various contrasted female figures in the story are drawn with an equally sympathetic and intelligent insight.'—*Scotsman.*

'Not a page of the book is dull.'—*Observer.*

'One loves it.'—*Evening Standard.*

THE CHEATS
By Marjorie Bowen
Author of *Mr Misfortunate*, etc.

7s. 6d. net

'Like the other romances of Miss Bowen, this book contains a number of powerfully and carefully drawn historical portraits and pictures.'—*Scotsman.*

'The general atmosphere of subterfuge and intrigue . . . which she depicts with her usual skill.'—*Times.*

Recent Publications

MARY-GIRL
By Hope Merrick   7s. net

'A powerful and original story . . . cleverly worked out.'—*Evening Standard*.

'Mary-Girl is real stuff, well told and well observed all through . . . well worth reading.'—*Observer*.

'Mrs Merrick's book is a real discovery . . . the sense of drama in the book is quite unusual . . . a singularly well written, well constructed and moving story.'—*Bookman*.

THE BANNER
By Hugh F. Spender
Author of *The Seekers*   7s. net

'A brilliant political fantasy.'—*Times*.

'Freshly written and well conceived.'—*Times Literary Supplement*.

'Decidedly clever.'—*Scotsman*.

POTTERISM
By Rose Macaulay
Author of *What Not*, etc.   7s. 6d. net

'A real achievement . . . the wittiest and most brilliant picture of present day life that has appeared for a long time.'—*Daily Chronicle*.

'A brilliant novel.'—*Observer*.

'Delicious humour . . . flashes of fun all through.'—Hamilton Fyfe in the *Daily Mail*.

Recent Publications

PANDORA'S YOUNG MEN
By Frederick Watson
Author of *The Humphries Touch*

7s. 6d. net

'A great wit . . . a brilliant and scintillating satire . . . delicious caricatures . . . the liveliest spirit of farce.'—*Daily Telegraph*.

'It makes you laugh (anyhow it made me laugh) suddenly, unexpectedly, and often.'—Rose Macaulay in the *Daily News*.

'For sheer wicked fun . . . one of the most frolicsome and chuckle-headed books ever written.'—Ralph Straus in the *Bystander*.

THE CLINTONS AND OTHERS
By Archibald Marshall
Author of *The Graftons*, etc.

7s. net

'Delightful, spirited, picturesque, and original.'—*Punch*.

'His talent in his own generation is unique, and no person who enjoys or studies the fiction of this age can afford to neglect it.'—*London Mercury*.

Recent Publications

THE SWORD OF LOVE
By Moray Dalton
Author of *Olive in Italy*

7s. *net*

'Skilfully contrived and excellently told.'—*Times.*

'A spirited performance, rich in incident and intrigue, and written by one who knows and loves Italy.'—*Spectator.*

THE DARK RIVER
By Sarah Gertrude Millin

6s. *net*

'She shapes a real story, sees real things, and real motives.'—*Daily News.*

'She writes almost like a Jane Austen of South Africa.'—*Land and Water.*

THE BOOK OF YOUTH
By Margaret Skelton

7s. 6d. *net*

'Margaret Skelton is a novelist of considerable possibilities, and this book in itself is a considerable achievement.'—*Times.*

Recent Publications

TWENTIETH CENTURY FRENCH WRITERS

By Madame Duclaux

Illustrated from Photographs

9s. net

'Charming essays, than which it is to be doubted whether there is any more attractive commentary either in English or in French, on their fascinating and provocative theme.'—*Bookman*.

'Truly delightful essays.'—*Morning Post*.

PATRICK SHAW-STEWART

By Ronald Knox

8s. net

'Admirably concise and vivid summaries . . . the book indicates the firm outline and the silver-lined shadows of a rare personality, *une intelligence d'élite*.'—*New Statesman*.

'Haunting biography . . . a supremely interesting sketch.'—*Outlook*.

Recent Publications

Books by Francis Brett Young

MARCHING ON TANGA
With General Smuts in East Africa

A NEW EDITION. *With Six Plates in Colour Numerous Illustrations in Black and White, Map, etc. Small Crown 4to. 10s. 6d. net*

'The best written of all the books produced during the war by men on active service. Its imaginative quality and charm of its style were no surprise to those who knew his early novels.'—*London Mercury*.

POEMS: 1916-1918
Large Crown 8vo. Boards. 5s. net

'Mr Brett Young is, in truth, if not one of the most nearly perfect, certainly one of the most interesting poets of to-day.'—*New Statesman*.

'It is unusual to find so much strength of thought, beauty of words, sincerity, imaginative vision, and technical accomplishment combined.'—Rose Macaulay in *Daily News*.

'Here, unless one is gravely mistaken, is something very like the real, imperishable thing.'—*Manchester Guardian*.

CAPTAIN SWING
A Romantic Play of 1830 in Four Acts
(Written in conjunction with W. Edward Stirling)
Crown 8vo. Paper. 2s. net

THE YOUNG PHYSICIAN
SECOND IMPRESSION 7s. net

'Giving us its author's best and placing him high indeed on the æsthetic plateau of performers in fiction.'—Thomas Seccombe in the *Daily Chronicle*.

'Lifted far above the average story in expression.'—*Morning Post*.

'One of the most vital stories ever written.'—*Illustrated London News*.

PR   Sinclair, May
6037   The romantic
I73R6

PLEASE DO NOT REMOVE
CARDS OR SLIPS FROM THIS POCKET

UNIVERSITY OF TORONTO LIBRARY

ImTheStory.com

Personalized Classic Books in many genre's

Unique gift for kids, partners, friends, colleagues

Customize:

- Character Names
- Upload your own front/back cover images (optional)
- Inscribe a personal message/dedication on the inside page (optional)

Customize many titles Including
- Alice in Wonderland
- Romeo and Juliet
- The Wizard of Oz
- A Christmas Carol
- Dracula
- Dr. Jekyll & Mr. Hyde
- And more...

Emily's Adventures in Wonderland

Ryan & Julia